MEDITATIONS ON ST. MATTHEW

by
Burns K. Seeley, Ph.D.

Nihil Obstat: Rev. John A. Hardon, S.J.
Censor Deputatus
Imprimatur: Rev. Msgr. John F. Donoghue
Vicar General of the Archdiocese of Washington, D.C.
November 5, 1981

Library of Congress Card Number 82-071700

ISBN Number 0-932406-05-X

Item number for this book is 323-76
The Apostolate, Box 220, Kenosha, WI 53141

File in
The Apostolate's Prayer Book
Book A4-1, Behind Section 2, Chapter 105

or

Living Meditation and Prayer Book Series
Book A4-3, Behind Section C2, Chapter 101

Structured by Jerome F. Coniker
Edited by Dale Francis

Published by
the Apostolate for Family Consecration
The Apostolate, Box 220
Kenosha, Wisconsin 53141

This book and the entire St. Matthew Peace of Heart Forums are dedicated to the Sorrowful and Immaculate Heart of Mary for the renewal of family life throughout the world.

Table of Contents

Act of Consecration

Heavenly Father, grant that we, who are nourished by the Body and Blood of Your Divine Son, may die to our own selfishness and be one spirit with Christ, as we seek to fulfill Your distinctive plan for our lives.

Form me and all the members of my family, community, and the Apostolate, into instruments of atonement. Unite our entire lives with the Holy Sacrifice of Jesus in the Mass of Calvary, and accept our seed sacrifice offering of all of our spiritual and material possessions, for the Sacred and Eucharistic Heart of Jesus, through the Sorrowful and Immaculate Heart of Mary, in union with St. Joseph.

Our Father, let Sacred Scripture's Four "C's" of Confidence, Conscience, seed-Charity, and Constancy, be our guide for living our consecration as peaceful children and purified instruments of the Most Holy Family.

Let us live our consecration by remaining perpetually confident, calm, cheerful, and compassionate, especially with the members of our own family and community.

Please protect our loved ones and ourselves from the temptations of the world, the flesh, and the devil. Help us to become more sensitive to the inspirations of Your Holy Spirit, the Holy Family, our Patron Saints, and Guardian Angels.

And now, Most Heavenly Father, inspire us

1

to establish the right priorities for Your precious gift of time. And most of all, help us to be more sensitive to the needs and feelings of our loved ones.

Never let us forget the souls in Purgatory who are dependent upon us for help. Enable us to gain, for the Poor Souls of our loved ones and others, as many indulgences as possible. We ask You this, Our Father, in the name of Our Lord and Savior Jesus Christ, Your Son and the Son of Mary. Amen.

Cenacle Prayer

(To Be Recited Before All AFC Gatherings)

Our Father, we gather together in the Name of Your Son Jesus Christ, and ask You to cast out all the demons coming against our families and the Apostolate for Family Consecration.

We entrust this gathering to the Sorrowful and Immaculate Heart of Mary, in union with St. Joseph. And through the intercession of our Patrons especially that of St. Vincent Pallotti, the Patron of all lay apostolates, we ask You to enable us, personally and collectively, to fulfill Your distinctive plan for our lives.

Father, we offer You the Precious Body, Blood, Soul and Divinity of Your Son, Our Lord Jesus Christ, in atonement for all of our sins and the sins of our families, neighborhoods, country and the entire world.

Most Holy Spirit, inspire, and protect us from pride, error and division. Bless our Holy Father the Pope, our Bishops and Priests. Also bless the activities and members of the Apostolate in this area.

Most Sacred and Eucharistic Heart of Jesus, pour Your Precious Blood down upon our families and the universal work of the Apostolate for Family Consecration. We particularly pray for the petitions placed at the foot of the Altar in our Sacred Hearts Chapel at the House of St. Joseph.

We ask all of this in Your Name, through the Immaculate Heart of our Mother Mary, in union with the Head of the Holy Family, St. Joseph. Amen.

Seed-Charity Prayer in the Spirit of St. Francis

Lord, make me an instrument of your peace;
Where there is hatred, let me sow seeds of love;
Where there is injury, let me sow seeds of pardon;
Where there is discord, let me sow seeds of union;
Where there is doubt, let me sow seeds of faith;
Where there is despair, let me sow seeds of hope;
Where there is darkness, let me sow seeds of light;
And where there is sadness, let me sow seeds of joy.
O Divine Master, grant that I may not so much seek to be consoled as to console You in others;
To be loved, as to love You in others;
For it is in *giving that we receive.*
It is in pardoning that we are pardoned,
And it is in *dying as a seed to our selfishness that we are born to eternal life.*

Prayer to St. Joseph for The Apostolate

St. Joseph, place me in the presence of the Blessed Sacrament of the altar in the Sacred Hearts Chapel, at the House of St. Joseph, and unite my prayers with those of the other members and friends of the society of the Apostolate for Family Consecration throughout the world.

We know, St. Joseph, that Our Lord will refuse you nothing. Please ask God to bless the Apostolate and all of its members and friends. Ask Our Lord to help the Apostolate accomplish its goal of establishing an international network of permanent chapters of dedicated volunteers. Ask Jesus to use these chapters to transform neighborhoods into God-centered communities by thoroughly educating people in the spiritual life.

St. Joseph, we are confident that you will remove all obstacles in the path of this spiritual renewal program, so that our society will be transformed through a chain reaction that will renew the family, the neighborhood, the school and the Church.

Form the society of the Apostolate for Family Consecration into a useful instrument of the Holy Family, and never let its members and leaders falsely judge others or fall into the sin of pride or complacency in success, which is so fatal to the work of God. Use the Apostolate as an instrument to bring about the social reign of the Sacred Heart of Jesus and the Immaculate Heart of Mary in our age. Amen.

Come Holy Spirit

Come, Holy Spirit, Who resides in the innermost recesses of my soul and give me the light of Your wisdom through the fire of Your divine love.

INTRODUCTION TO ST. MATTHEW
by
Burns K. Seeley, Ph.D.

1. Before you begin meditating on St. Matthew's Gospel, please take time to read these introductory pages. They will help you cultivate the art of meditation.

2. When meditating on Matthew, and on other portions of Scripture, we want you to discover for yourselves Scripture's Four C's Formula for Peaceful Seed Living. It is a formula which will enable you to rise above your problems and accomplish worthy goals you never thought possible. It will also enable you to help countless suffering souls on earth

and in Purgatory. Therefore, we are first going to spend a few minutes discussing this formula, concentrating on the nature of each of the Four C's.

3.   Then, we will share with you some suggestions on how to meditate well. This will be followed by some background material on St. Matthew and his Gospel, which will help you better understand the man and the message he conveys as Christ's Apostle and Evangelist.

Scripture's Four C's

4.   What are Scripture's Four C's? Those of you who are already acquainted with the work of the Apostolate for Family Consecration will no doubt already know the answer, especially if you have read Volume I of Jerome Coniker's two volume work called "Scripture's Four C's Formula for Peaceful Seed Living" and his "Prayers and Recommended Practices" book. *(For information on the work and goals of the Apostolate see pp. 252.)*

5.   Confidence, Conscience, seed-Charity and Constancy. These are the four pillars of the *Peaceful Seed-Living Formula.* And, we hope they will become a permanent part of your lives so you will always have ready access to that God-given peace which defies complete understanding.

Confidence (C-1)

6.   The first C - "Confidence." When we speak of "Confidence," what do we mean? We mean a supernaturally-given trust in God,

a trust in His unique plan for each of us, and a trust in the strength He will give us to accomplish this plan. Since God is completely good, He desires only what is best for us, namely, our interior peace. But if we are to obtain this inner peace of heart, our trust or confidence, must be focused on Him.

7. We also mean by confidence, a supernaturally-given ability to believe the truths which the Father has revealed for our salvation through the patriarchs, the prophets, the Apostles, and especially through Jesus. When we use confidence to mean this type of belief, we are using it in the same way that "faith" is used in most of the New Testament, this is, in the exclusively Christian part of the Bible.

8. Less frequently, we use confidence to mean hope, that is, hope in eternal life with God, hope in the rewards that accompany eternal life and hope in the means of obtaining it.

9. It can be seen then, that we use confidence as a synonym for trust, faith and hope, which are special graces, mentioned often in the New Testament, and given by God for our salvation.

10. To sum up, The Apostolate speaks of confidence as trust in God, belief in His supernaturally revealed truths, hope in eternal life, and hope in the means to obtain it.

Conscience (C-2)
11. Now, the second C - "Conscience." As

used by the Apostolate for Family Consecration, conscience means a pure conscience, or one that is free from all fully deliberate sins, since these are the major obstacles to spiritual growth and a life of union or oneness with God.

12.   Imperfections and half deliberate sins, on the other hand, while they do not prevent us from enjoying God's friendship and a pure conscience, are nonetheless obstacles to obtaining a purer conscience, and can therefore be sources of spiritual illnesses leading to mortal sins. Consequently, we should, with the aid of God's grace, seek to remove them, too, along with all willfull sins.

13.   Through Scripture, we are counselled to purify our consciences by repenting of our sins so we can grow in holiness and in God's friendship. In order to accomplish this properly, a daily in-depth self-examination for these hindrances to holiness should be undertaken.

14. Next, our third C - "seed-Charity." Seed-charity or seed-sacrifice, or we could say seed-love, is that grace referred to in the Bible which makes it possible for us to offer ourselves fully to the true service of God and our fellow man. Put another way, we could say seed-charity enables us to love God as He commanded us to do with all our hearts, with all our souls, with all our minds, and with all our strength, and to love our neighbor as ourselves. Indeed, seed-charity enables us to love others as Christ has loved us, that is, even to the point of death.

15. We of the Apostolate prefer the term "seed-charity" to simply "charity" or "love," since in modern English it is not always clear what these latter two terms mean. Thus when we prefix "seed" to charity, we wish to convey the idea of a love which is essentially sacrificial. Without this prefix, charity is often thought of solely in terms of donating time or money to some worthy cause. But activity of this sort is not always sacrificial. Also, the word "love" without the prefix "seed" could mean either romantic love or the love of casual friendship, but neither of these needs to be sacrificial either.

16. If we were to reflect on it, we would all realize a seed is meant to sacrifice itself, or die, so a new life, that of a plant, might slowly emerge and eventually achieve full growth. Similarly, one who exercises sacrificial love or seed-charity dies to his selfishness, so a new Christ-like individual can emerge and ulti-

mately attain full growth in sanctity through a transforming union with Our Lord.

17.   We do not have to look further than our own immediate environment to know where we should plant our seeds of sacrificial charity. And in doing so, we are faithfully fulfilling our responsibilities in our state in life. Trials, for instance, which come upon all of us, can be sanctified by offering them to God in the spirit of seed-charity. When we plant seeds of sacrifice to meet our spiritual needs in this life, we are preparing ourselves for eternal life with God in His heavenly Kingdom. We are also achieving *peaceful seed-living* on earth, and we are having our material and emotional needs met as well.

Constancy (C-4)

18. Finally, the fourth C - "Constancy." By constancy we mean a special supernatural grace which allows us to persevere with a pure conscience in the Christian life, even during moments of difficult temptations. We need this grace to persevere in all acts which lead to our destiny in Heaven, but especially in the exercise of confidence and seed-charity.

19. Constancy is living in God's presence. It is a constant vigilance always to do the things that please God. This includes maintaining a positive attitude of expectation for God's love, for responses to our prayers, and for God's harvest from the charitable seeds we have planted. In a certain sense we cay say constancy is the most important of all virtues, since it undergirds and reinforces all the others. Without it, all of our efforts would bear little spiritual fruit.

The Four C's

20. Now let's condense and simplify our definitions of the Four C's. Confidence refers to those graces which make it possible for us to trust and hope in God, and also to believe all the truths He has revealed supernaturally for our salvation.

21. By conscience, we normally mean a conscience which is pure or free of all fully deliberate sins and aware of one's faults to be overcome.

22. Seed-charity is the supernatural ability to sacrifice ourselves for God by loving Him

directly through prayer and worship, and also in our neighbor. We love God too by fulfilling our responsibilities and changing our trials into positive seeds of sacrifice.

23. Finally, there is constancy which is a special God-given aid that helps us persevere in the fulfillment of our Christian responsibilities and be alert to God's harvest sent our way to fulfill our needs so we can do His will on earth and finally obtain Heaven.

Meditation

24. Making good meditations is crucial for proper spiritual development. That is why they are an integral part of the Apostolate's spiritual leadership programs.

25. In general, we could say that a spiritual meditation consists simply in making a prayerful reflection on some spiritual topic or topics with the purpose of knowing and loving God better.

26.   Sacred Scripture or, for that matter, any number of excellent spiritual books, can serve as focal points for meditating since they are rich sources of spiritual subject matter. We would recommend first and foremost, however, the use of Sacred Scripture, inasmuch as it is the primary source book of Christian spirituality.

27.   Over the centuries, the Church has highly recommended scriptural meditation. The Second Vatican Council (1962-1965), for example, spoke of scriptural meditation as a means of dialoguing with God. Thus it noted that we speak to God when we pray and we listen to Him when we read (and meditate on) His written Word. *("Dogmatic Constitution on Divine Revelation," #25.)*

28.   What are the main steps in a scriptural meditation? First, a quiet place should be found — ideally in a church in the presence of the Blessed Sacrament. But, for many, this may not be practical on a regular basis. Consequently, you might choose an isolated area in your home, such as a bedroom.

29.   It would be helpful to start your meditation with a prayer to Mary, the Spouse of the Holy Spirit, for help in making your meditation fruitful. And if you have not already done so, it would be well to examine your conscience and confess your sins so there will be no obstacles to the action of God's grace within you. One more thing — it is best to meditate at the same time each day. This makes it easier for meditation to become a habit and, therefore, a normal part of your life.

30.   Now, placing the Scripture reading you are going to meditate on in front of you, you should be ready to begin. It is best to read slowly and deliberately, and if you feel moved to do so, to pause from time to time, to reflect on the sentences or passage just read.

31.   What do they mean? What is God saying to you and to your families through them? What acts of charity do they suggest? Perhaps they suggest more fervent prayers, or greater generosity to those closest to you, or some special act of seed-charity for someone you have wrongfully injured.

32.   Also when meditating try to find within the Scripture readings, words and ideas which suggest the Four C's. You will probably be surprised to see how often they occur. Confidence, as we have already mentioned, can be seen in words such as "faith," "hope" and "trust." Conscience, or a pure conscience, is suggested immediately by terms such as a "pure heart," and an "honest

16

and good heart." And it is suggested indirectly by many references to sins which must be repented of before a pure conscience can be secured. The idea of seed-charity is found especially in the frequent use of "love" — and the concept of constancy can be found in the use of words such as "persevere" and "endure."

33. Note also in the margin of your Scripture readings, the numbered C's. C-1 represents confidence. C-2 stands for conscience. C-3 stands for seed-charity, C-4 represents constancy, and C-5 represents a combination of the Four C's. These are guides for you in discovering the Four C's in the adjacent Scripture passages. You will undoubtedly discover other references to them as well.

34. It is important that your meditations be forms of prayer, and the subject matter of each prayer should be whatever the Holy Spirit suggests to you while meditating. Perhaps you will be led to express sorrow for your sins, or gratitude for having a loving God Who was willing to become man to suffer and die for each of us. Or reflecting on Scripture may bring to mind those who could use your prayers and other sacrificial acts.

35. During the three weeks of the present spiritual formation program, when you have completed your daily meditation on Scripture, read the prepared companion meditation in the same slow, deliberate manner. This is found immediately following the Scripture reading.

36. The purpose of using the companion meditations is to give you additional insights into the meaning of God's written word for yourself, your family and others.

37. We suggest that if you have not meditated regularly before that, at first, you spend only fifteen to twenty mintes a day in meditation. Then we recommend you work your way up to a half hour and then perhaps to an hour, both of which will quite likely seem to pass rather quickly. Set your own pace and ask Mary, the Spouse of the Holy Spirit, to take you by the hand and lead you into the spiritual life.

38. Now for a few words about St. Matthew and the Gospel that bears his name.

St. Matthew

39. As you may already know, St. Matthew, or Levi, was one of Jesus' twelve Apostles.

Formerly, he had been a Jewish publican or tax collector.

40. The publicans as a group were despised by most Jews on account of their close relationship with the Roman authorities for whom they worked, and because they often abused their office by collecting unjust sums of money.

41. Despite Matthew's notorious position, Our Lord perceived his potential for sanctity and for leadership in the Church. It should not be surprising then, that he should have been called to serve as an Apostle.

42. Although some modern Scripture scholars have questioned whether Matthew was indeed the author of this Gospel, the earliest historical evidence and the constant tradition of the Catholic Church affirm that he was.

43. It may be of interest to know that the word "gospel" comes from an old English term meaning glad tidings or good news. Thus we could refer to St. Matthew's Gospel as his version of the Good News of man's salvation.

44. Also the Greek word for good news is *evangelion*. It is from this term that we get "evangelist" or one who spreads the Good News of salvation.

St. Matthew's Gospel

45. St. Matthew wrote his version of the Gospel for the Jews of Palestine. The chief reason for doing so was to persuade them

Jesus was the long-awaited Christ or Messiah,
Who had come to save them from their sins.

46. St. Matthew also wished to convince
the Jews that the crucified and risen Jesus
had established the Kingdom of Heaven, or
the Church, on earth. It was this messianic
Kingdom of the New Covenant which was
intended to replace God's ancient Kingdom
of Israel and the Old Covenant, which were
only temporary and preparatory in nature.
*(For a discussion of the Church as the Kingdom of
Heaven on earth see Father John A. Hardon's "The
Catholic Catechism," Doubleday and Co., N.Y. pp.
208-209.)*

47. When compared to the other Gospel
accounts written by Saints Mark, Luke and
John, St. Matthew's version can be seen to
give us the most complete picture of Jesus'
life and doctrine, although each of these other
versions has its own distinctive contributions
to make as well.

48. St. Matthew divided his Gospel into

three principal sections. First, he gives an account of Jesus' conception and birth, and the events surrounding them. Secondly, the public ministry of Our Lord is described. This being by far the longest section. Finally, there are the accounts of Jesus' suffering or Passion, His death on the Cross, and His bodily Resurrection from the dead.

49. In summary, we can say this version of the Gospel was written for Palestinian Jews by St. Matthew the Apostle. His chief purpose in writing was to convince the Jews that the crucified and resurrected Jesus of Nazareth was the Messiah Who brought into existence on earth His long-expected Kingdom. St. Matthew's Gospel consists of three main sections: the first deals with Jesus' conception, birth and infancy; the second touches on His public ministry; and the third pertains to His Passion, Crucifixion and Resurrection.

50. As you meditate on St. Matthew's Gospel during the next three weeks, we hope God will richly bless you, drawing you ever closer to Him.

"Peaceful Seed Living"
Prayer and Meditation Book, Volume II

51.　At the end of each of the companion meditations, which follow the daily Scripture selections, note the references to Volume II of the "Peaceful Seed Living" prayer and meditation book. Be sure to read them. These will give you further insights into the spirituality of the Apostolate for Family Consecration, including the spirituality of consecration and that of the Scripture's Four C's. You will also receive information about the structure of the Apostolate. This small book, features Mother Teresa of Calcutta's own meditations and Father John A. Hardon's theological talk on the Apostolate's Scripture's Four C's spirituality.

"The Catholic Catechism"
by Fr. John A. Hardon, S.J.

52.　You will find many references throughout the following meditations to Father John A. Hardon's "The Catholic Catechism" published by Doubleday and Co., N.Y. This handbook on our Faith is one of the most thorough and concise books of its kind. If you want to get the most out of your meditations, we strongly recommend that you obtain a copy of this book and refer to it as we specify sections from it throughout this text. As Scripture unfolds our Faith, Father Hardon's "The Catholic Catechism" will give you an indepth knowledge of it in a very quick and easy way. If you wish, you may order a copy from the Apostolate, Box 220, Kenosha, WI 53141.

"Modern Catholic Dictionary"
by Fr. John A. Hardon, S.J.

53.   Also referred to in the following meditations are entries from Fr. Hardon's "Modern Catholic Dictionary," also published by Doubleday and Co., N.Y. This scholarly work serves as a handy reference book featuring thousands of short, easy-to-read, entries on religious topics, including those widely mentioned and discussed since the Second Vatican Council. This, too, can be purchased from the Apostolate.

Neighborhood Peace of Heart Forums

54.   While this book on St. Matthew's Gospel can be read as a complete unit in itself, it was primarily designed to be a meditation book for one of the Apostolate for Family Consecration's Neighborhood Peace of Heart Forums, forums conducted by authorized Neighborhood Chapters of the Apostolate. A Peace of Heart Forum consists of four meetings, over a 22-day period, in private homes for small gatherings of neighbors who come together to view the Apostolate's home videotape television programs and participate in discussing the spiritual truths they have read about and meditated on.

55.   If you would like to attend a Neighborhood Peace of Heart Forum, or help form a Neighborhood Chapter in your area, please contact us at the AFC, Box 220, Kenosha, WI 53141.

56. The specific purpose of the Apostolate is to utilize programs like this to transform neighborhoods into God-centered communities, communities supportive of the sacredness of family life.

THE GOSPEL

ACCORDING TO

Saint Matthew

I. THE BIRTH AND INFANCY OF JESUS

The ancestry of Jesus

1 **1** A genealogy of Jesus Christ, son of David, son of Abraham:[a]

2 Abraham was the father of Isaac,
Isaac the father of Jacob,
Jacob the father of Judah and his brothers,
3 Judah was the father of Perez and Zerah,
Tamar being their mother,
Perez was the father of Hezron,
Hezron the father of Ram,
4 Ram was the father of Amminadab,
Amminadab the father of Nahshon,
Nahshon the father of Salmon,
5 Salmon was the father of Boaz, Rahab being his mother,
Boaz was the father of Obed, Ruth being his mother,
Obed was the father of Jesse;
6 and Jesse was the father of King David.
David was the father of Solomon, whose mother had been Uriah's wife,
7 Solomon was the father of Rehoboam,

Rehoboam the father of Abijah,
Abijah the father of Asa,

8 Asa was the father of Jehoshaphat,
Jehoshaphat the father of Joram,
Joram the father of Azariah,

9 Azariah was the father of Jotham,
Jotham the father of Ahaz,
Ahaz the father of Hezekiah,

10 Hezekiah was the father of Manasseh,
Manasseh the father of Amon,
Amon the father of Josiah;

11 and Josiah was the father of Jechoniah and
his brothers.
Then the deportation to Babylon took place.

12 After the deportation to Babylon:
Jechoniah was the father of Shealtiel,
Shealtiel the father of Zerubbabel,

13 Zerubbabel was the father of Abiud,
Abiud the father of Eliakim,
Eliakim the father of Azor,

14 Azor was the father of Zadok,
Zadok the father of Achim,
Achim the father of Eliud,

15 Eliud was the father of Eleazar,
Eleazar the father of Matthan,
Matthan the father of Jacob;

16 and Jacob was the father of Joseph the husband of Mary;
of her was born Jesus who is called Christ.

17 The sum of generations is therefore: fourteen from Abraham to David; fourteen from David to the Babylonian deportation; and fourteen from the Babylonian deportation to Christ.

The virginal conception of Christ

18 This is how Jesus Christ came to be born. His mother Mary was betrothed to Joseph;*b* (C2) but before they came to live together she was found to be with child through the Holy
19 Spirit. •Her husband Joseph, being a man of (C2) honor and wanting to spare her publicity, de- (C3)
20 cided to divorce her informally. •He had made up his mind to do this when the angel of the Lord appeared to him in a dream and said, "Joseph son of David, do not be afraid to take Mary home as your wife, because she has conceived what is in her by the Holy
21 Spirit. •She will give birth to a son and you must name him Jesus, because he is the one who is to save*c* his people from
22 their sins." •Now all this took place to fulfill the words spoken by the Lord through the prophet:

23 *The virgin will conceive and give birth to a son and they will call him Immanuel,d*

a name which means "God-is-with-us."
24 When Joseph woke up he did what the angel (C1) of the Lord had told him to do: he took his (C3)
25 wife to his home •and, though he had not had intercourse with her, she gave birth to a son; and he named him Jesus.

The visit of the Magi

1 2 After Jesus had been born at Bethlehem in Judaea during the reign of King Herod,*a* some wise men came to Jerusalem from
2 the east. •"Where is the infant king of the Jews?" they asked. "We saw his star as it (C3) rose*b* and have come to do him homage."

3 When King Herod heard this he was per-
turbed, and so was the whole of Jerusalem. (C2)
4 He called together all the chief priests and
the scribes of the people, and enquired of
5 them where the Christ was to be born. •"At
Bethlehem in Judaea," they told him "for this
is what the prophet wrote:

6 *And you, Bethlehem, in the land of Judah,*
you are by no means least among the leaders
of Judah,
for out of you will come a leader
*who will shepherd my people Israel."*ᶜ

7 Then Herod summoned the wise men to see
him privately. He asked them the exact date
8 on which the star had appeared, •and sent
them on to Bethlehem. "Go and find out all
about the child," he said "and when you have
found him, let me know, so that I too may
9 go and do him homage." •Having listened to
what the king had to say, they set out. And
there in front of them was the star they had
seen rising; it went forward and halted over
10 the place where the child was. •The sight of
11 the star filled them with delight, •and going
into the house they saw the child with his

28

mother Mary, and falling to their knees they (C3)
did him homage. Then, opening their treasures, they offered him gifts of gold and (C3)
12 frankincense and myrrh.*d* •But they were
warned in a dream not to go back to Herod,
and returned to their own country by a differ- (C1)
ent way. (C3)

The flight into Egypt. The massacre of the Innocents

13   After they had left, the angel of the Lord
appeared to Joseph in a dream and said, "Get
up, take the child and his mother with you,
and escape into Egypt, and stay there until
I tell you, because Herod intends to search
14 for the child and do away with him." •So (C1)
Joseph got up and, taking the child and his (C3)
mother with him, left that night for Egypt,
15 where he stayed until Herod was dead. This
was to fulfill what the Lord had spoken
through the prophet:

*I called my son out of Egypt.*e

16   Herod was furious when he realized that (C2)
he had been outwitted by the wise men, and
in Bethlehem and its surrounding district he
had all the male children killed who were two
years old or under, reckoning by the date he
17 had been careful to ask the wise men. •It was
then that the words spoken through the
prophet Jeremiah were fulfilled:

18   *A voice was heard in Ramah,*
    sobbing and loudly lamenting:
    it was Rachel weeping for her children,
    refusing to be comforted
    *because they were no more.*f

From Egypt to Nazareth

19   After Herod's death, the angel of the Lord
20 appeared in a dream to Joseph in Egypt •and
said, "Get up, take the child and his mother
with you and go back to the land of Israel, (C1)
for those who wanted to kill the child are

29

21 dead." •So Joseph got up and, taking the (C3)
child and his mother with him, went back to
22 the land of Israel. •But when he learned that
Archelaus^g had succeeded his father Herod
as ruler of Judaea he was afraid to go there,
and being warned in a dream he left for the (C1)
23 region of Galilee.^h •There he settled in a town (C3)
called Nazareth. In this way the words spo-
ken through the prophets were to be fulfilled:

He will be called a Nazarene.

Week 1 Day 1
Four C's Meditations
on St. Matthew 1:1-2:23

1. Our Father in Heaven, as we reflected in
today's reading on the birth of Jesus and the
events surrounding it, the dangers the Holy
Family faced became quite apparent. It was
quickly brought to our attention, however,
that You were also there protecting Mary and
Joseph and the Baby Jesus so Your plan for
our salvation would not be hindered. We
observed too that during those early days in

the life of the Holy Family, St. Joseph played an especially important role as the guardian of Jesus and Mary, since he was Jesus' foster father and Mary's true husband.

2. At first, of course, Joseph was ignorant of the great privilege of being chosen to be the foster father of the Messiah. Thus, when he learned, before living with Mary, that she was bearing a child, he was understandably troubled and confused. But You spoke to him through an angel to assure him Mary's child was miraculously conceived by God the Holy Spirit. For that reason, You told him, he should not hesitate to live with her.

3. We noted that Joseph immediately responded according to Your will, thus reflecting his belief and trust in You. Moreover, his act of obedience was an act of self-sacrifice, since he first wanted to leave Mary quietly, thereby sparing her a great deal of embarrassment and even the likelihood that she would be put to death for an alleged adulterous affair. Undoubtedly, in conforming to Your will — which was an act of seed-charity — St. Joseph found that peace of heart which You alone can give in the midst of trials. *(According to the Old Testament Law, adultery was punishable by death. See Leviticus 20:10.)*

4. Again, when Joseph obeyed Your command to take the Holy Family into Egypt, and when he later followed Your directive to return to Palestine with Our Lady and Jesus, he also exercised confidence (belief and trust) in You, as well as seed-charity. Moreover, his

repeated acts of faith, trust and seed-charity revealed the virtue of constancy.

5. What a contrast, Most Loving Father, between St. Joseph and King Herod! While Joseph found Your comforting peace in the midst of poverty and hardships, Herod, the powerful and rich ruler, experienced only unhappiness and grief, since he favored his will instead of Yours.

6. Lord, in today's meditation, we also observed Your providential action in the lives of the wise men, who were led by a star to the manger in Bethlehem. Like St. Joseph, they too evidenced a conscience sensitive to Your will. This was seen, especially, in their desire to worship the infant Redeemer, which in fact was fulfilled as they knelt before the Babe in the presence of Mary and Joseph.

7. Heavenly Father, may we daily follow the saintly example of St. Joseph.

Particularly, may we imitate his deep love for You while worshipping You at Mass and in our prayers. We ask this through Jesus Christ, Our Lord, to Whom, with You and the Holy Spirit be all honor and glory. Amen.

Try to read these Scripture passages and meditations several times a day in a reflective manner. Each time you do so, the Holy Spirit will give you more insights. (Some families read them together once a day and privately at another time during the day.)

Read and meditate on Chapter X, Paragraphs 1 to 8 in our "Peaceful Seed Living" book, Volume II.

II. THE KINGDOM OF HEAVEN PROCLAIMED

A. NARRATIVE SECTION

The preaching of John the Baptist

1 **3** In due course John the Baptist appeared;
he preached in the wilderness of Judaea
2 and this was his message: •"Repent, for the   (C2)
3 kingdom of heaven*a* is close at hand." •This
was the man the prophet Isaiah spoke of
when he said:

> *A voice cries in the wilderness:*
> *Prepare a way for the Lord,*
> *make his paths straight.*[b]

4 This man John wore a garment made of cam-
el-hair with a leather belt round his waist, and
5 his food was locusts and wild honey. •Then
Jerusalem and all Judaea and the whole Jor-
6 dan district made their way to him, •and as
they were baptized by him in the river Jordan
7 they confessed their sins. •But when he saw
a number of Pharisees and Sadducees*c* com-
8 ing for baptism he said to them, •"Brood of   (C2)
vipers, who warned you to fly from the retri-
bution that is coming? But if you are repent-   (C2)
9 ant, produce the appropriate fruit, •and do not
presume to tell yourselves, 'We have Abraham for our father,' because, I tell you, God
can raise children for Abraham from these
10 stones. •Even now the ax is laid to the roots
of the trees, so that any tree which fails to   (C2)
produce good fruit will be cut down and
11 thrown on the fire. •I baptize you in water for   (C2)

34

repentance, but the one who follows me is more powerful than I am, and I am not fit to carry his sandals; he will baptize you with the 12 Holy Spirit and fire. •His winnowing-fan is in his hand; he will clear his threshing-floor and gather his wheat into the barn; but the chaff he will burn in a fire that will never go out."

Jesus is baptized

13 Then Jesus appeared: he came from Galilee 14 to the Jordan to be baptized by John.•John (C1) tried to dissuade him. "It is I who need bap- (C2) tism from you," he said, "and yet you come 15 to me!" •But Jesus replied, "Leave it like this for the time being; it is fitting that we should, in this way, do all that righteousness demands." At this, John gave in to (C3) him.

16 As soon as Jesus was baptized he came up from the water, and suddenly the heavens opened and he saw the Spirit of God descending like a dove and coming down on 17 him. •And a voice spoke from heaven, "This is my Son, the Beloved; my favor rests on him."

Temptation in the wilderness

1 **4** Then Jesus was led by the Spirit out into the wilderness to be tempted by the devil. (C2)
2 He fasted for forty days and forty nights, after 3 which he was very hungry, •and the tempter came and said to him, "If you are the Son of God, tell these stones to turn into loaves." (C2)
4 But he replied, "Scripture says:

Man does not live on bread alone
but on every word that comes from the mouth
of God."ᵃ

5 The devil then took him to the holy city and made him stand on the parapet of the Tem-
6 ple. •"If you are the Son of God" he said (C2) "throw yourself down; for scripture says:

35

He will put you in his angels' charge,
and they will support you on their hands
in case you hurt your foot against a stone."[b]

7 Jesus said to him, "Scripture also says:

You must not put the Lord your God to the
test."[c]

8 Next, taking him to a very high mountain, the
devil showed him all the kingdoms of the (C2)
9 world and their splendor. •"I will give you all
these" he said, "if you fall at my feet and
10 worship me." •Then Jesus replied, "Be off,
Satan! For scripture says:

You must worship the Lord your God,
and serve him alone."[d]

11 Then the devil left him, and angels appeared
and looked after him. (C3)

Return to Galilee

12 Hearing that John had been arrested he
13 went back to Galilee, ·and leaving Nazareth
he went and settled in Capernaum, a lakeside
town on the borders of Zebulun and Naph-
14 tali. ·In this way the prophecy of Isaiah was
to be fulfilled:

15 *Land of Zebulun! Land of Naphtali!*
Way of the sea on the far side of Jordan;
Galilee of the nations!
16 *The people that lived in darkness*
has seen a great light;
on those who dwell in the land and shadow
of death
*a light has dawned.*e

17 From that moment Jesus began his preaching (C1)
with the message, "Repent, for the kingdom
of heaven is close at hand." (C2)

The first four disciples are called

18 As he was walking by the Sea of Galilee
he saw two brothers, Simon, who was called
Peter, and his brother Andrew; they were
making a cast in the lake with their net, for
19 they were fishermen. ·And he said to them,
"Follow me and I will make you fishers of
20 men." ·And they left their nets at once and (C1)
followed him. (C3)
21 Going on from there he saw another pair
of brothers, James son of Zebedee and his
brother John; they were in their boat with
their father Zebedee, mending their nets, and
22 he called them. ·At once, leaving the boat and
their father, they followed him.

Jesus preaches and heals the sick

23 He went round the whole of Galilee teaching in their synagogues, proclaiming the
Good News of the kingdo. . and curing all (C3)
kinds of diseases and sickness among the
24 people. ·His fame spread throughout Syria,f

37

and those who were suffering from diseases and painful complaints of one kind or another, the possessed, epileptics, the paralyzed, were all brought to him, and he cured (C3)
25 them. •Large crowds followed him, coming from Galilee, the Decapolis,*g* Jerusalem, Judaea and Transjordania.

Week 1 Day 2
Four C's Meditations
on St. Matthew 3:1-4:25

1. Lord Jesus, when meditating on today's Scripture reading, our need for repentance became abundantly clear. How frail and weak we are. How often we turn away from You, the Source of all true happiness, goodness and peace. Lord, forgive us all our sins so our hearts might once more be pure. Especially forgive us those sins which have offended both You and the members of our families. Furthermore, since Christian families are the

basic cells of Your Mystical Body, the Church, our offenses against them, in one way or another, harm the effectiveness of Your Church, which exists as Your instrument to save the world.

2. Help us, too, Jesus, to follow the example of Your cousin, John the Baptist. With humble submissiveness, he deferred to Your will when You insisted on being baptized by him. In this act of humility, he died to himself, spiritually speaking, and experienced the supernatural life of Your grace which prepared him for life in Your eternal Kingdom. *(For a discussion of the supernatural life of grace, read pp. 177-178 of "The Catholic Catechism.")*

3. In the accounts of Your temptations in the wilderness, Most Merciful Lord, we saw Your perseverance in resisting the attractions of that great deceiver, satan. Since as Your followers, we too are tempted by the demonic, may the power of Your Holy Spirit enable us to recognize satan's presence and activity, as well as that of his fellow demons. And may we, like You, resist them all through the graces You give us in the sacraments and in prayer. *(For further information on satan and his temptations, read pp. 87-90 of "The Catholic Catechism.")*

4. We also noticed in our meditation, Most Sacred Heart of Jesus, the confidence (belief and trust), and seed-charity of Your Apostles, Peter, Andrew, James and John. Although they hardly knew You at the time, Your presence and words were enough to convince

them You were worthy of their belief and trust. Their immediate acceptance of Your command to follow You and leave behind their accustomed livelihood marked the beginning of their lives of conscious self-sacrifice for You. Also, through their self-sacrifice or seed-charity, they were retaining and developing the immeasurable gift of Your friendship with its accompanying inner peace.

5. O merciful Savior, help us to turn to You daily in faith and in trust, and inspire us to plant seeds of charity so we may please You and store up for ourselves treasures in Heaven. *(1)*

6.   Finally, Lord, inspire us to act each day in concert with Your eternal plan for us, and may we, as individuals and families, constantly seek the powerful protection of the Holy Family as an aid to our growth in holiness.

7.   "All for the Sacred and Eucharistic Heart of Jesus. All through the Sorrowful and Immaculate Heart of Mary and all in union with St. Joseph. This shall be our commitment in life, in death and in eternity." Amen.

Try to read these Scripture passages and meditations in a reflective manner more than once a day. The Holy Spirit will reveal more insights to you each time you do so.

Please read and meditate on Chapter X, Paragraphs 9 to 22 of the "Peaceful Seed Living" prayer and meditation book, Volume II.

B. THE SERMON ON THE MOUNT[a]

The Beatitudes

1 **5** Seeing the crowds, he went up the hill.
There he sat down and was joined by his
2 disciples. ·Then he began to speak. This is
what he taught them:

3 "How happy are the poor in spirit;   (C2)
theirs is the kingdom of heaven.

4 Happy *the gentle:*[b]   (C2)
they shall have the earth for their heritage.

5 Happy those who mourn: (C3)
they shall be comforted.

6 Happy those who hunger and thirst for what   (C2)
is right:
they shall be satisfied.

7 Happy the merciful: (C2)
they shall have mercy shown them.

8 Happy the pure in heart: (C2)
they shall see God.

9 Happy the peacemakers: (C3)
they shall be called sons of God.

10 Happy those who are persecuted in the cause (C2)
of right:
theirs is the kingdom of heaven.   (C3)

11 "Happy are you when people abuse you and   (C2)
persecute you and speak all kinds of calumny

12 against you on my account. ·Rejoice and be   (C3)
glad, for your reward will be great in heaven;
this is how they persecuted the prophets   (C2)
before you.

13 "You are the salt of the earth. But if salt ⁽ᶜ²⁾ becomes tasteless, what can make it salty again? It is good for nothing, and can only be thrown out to be trampled underfoot by men.

14 "You are the light of the world. A city built ⁽ᶜ²⁾
15 on a hill-top cannot be hidden. ·No one lights a lamp to put it under a tub; they put it on the lamp-stand where it shines for everyone
16 in the house. ·In the same way your light must shine in the sight of men, so that, seeing your good works, they may give the praise to your Father in heaven.

The fulfillment of the Law

17 "Do not imagine that I have come to abolish the Law or the Prophets. I have come not
18 to abolish but to complete them. ·I tell you ⁽ᶜ³⁾ solemnly, till heaven and earth disappear, not one dot, not one little stroke, shall disappear from the Law until its purpose is achieved.
19 Therefore, the man who infringes even one ⁽ᶜ²⁾ of the least of these commandments and teaches others to do the same will be considered the least in the kingdom of heaven; but the man who keeps them and teaches them **will be considered great in the kingdom of** ⁽ᶜ³⁾ **heaven.** ⁽ᶜ⁴⁾

43

20   "For I tell you, if your virtue goes no (C2)
deeper than that of the scribes and Pharisees,
you will never get into the kingdom of
heaven.

21   "You have learned how it was said to our
ancestors: *You must not kill;c* and if anyone (C2)
does kill he must answer for it before the

22 court. •But I say this to you: anyone who is
angry with his brother will answer for it (C2)
before the court; if a man calls his brother
'Fool'*d* he will answer for it before the Sanhe- (C2)
drin;*e* and if a man calls him 'Renegade'*f* he

23 will answer for it in hell fire. •So then, if you (C2)
are bringing your offering to the altar and
there remember that your brother has some-

24 thing against you, •leave your offering there (C2)
before the altar, go and be reconciled with (C3)
your brother first, and then come back and (C3)

25 present your offering. •Come to terms with
your opponent in good time while you are
still on the way to the court with him, or he
may hand you over to the judge and the judge
to the officer, and you will be thrown into

26 prison. •I tell you solemnly, you will not get
out till you have paid the last penny.

27   "You have learned how it was said: *You* (C2)
28 *must not commit adultery.g* •But I say this to
you: if a man looks at a woman lustfully, he (C2)
has already committed adultery with her in

29 his heart. •If your right eye should cause you
to sin, tear it out and throw it away; for it will
do you less harm to lose one part of you than
to have your whole body thrown into hell.

30 And if your right hand should cause you to
sin, cut if off and throw it away; for it will do
you less harm to lose one part of you than
to have your whole body go to hell.

31   "It has also been said: *Anyone who divorces his wife must give her a writ of dis-*
32 *missal.h* •But I say this to you: everyone who
divorces his wife, except for the case of for- (C2)

44

nication, makes her an adulteress; and anyone who marries a divorced woman commits (C2) adultery.

33 "Again, you have learned how it was said to our ancestors: *You must not break your oath, but must fulfill your oaths to the Lord.*[i]
34 But I say this to you: do not swear at all, either by *heaven*, since that is God's throne; (C2)
35 or by *the earth*, since that is *his footstool;* or by Jerusalem, since that is *the city of the great*
36 *king.* •Do not swear by your own head either, (C2) since you cannot turn a single hair white or (C2)
37 black. •All you need say is 'Yes' if you mean (C2) yes, 'No' if you mean no; anything more than this comes from the evil one. (C2)

38 "You have learned how it was said: *Eye for*
39 *eye and tooth for tooth.*[j] •But I say this to you: (C2) offer the wicked man no resistance. On the (C3) contrary, if anyone hits you on the right
40 cheek, offer him the other as well; •if a man (C3) takes you to law and would have your tunic, (C3)
41 let him have your cloak as well. •And if anyone orders you to go one mile, go two miles (C3)
42 with him. •Give to anyone who asks, and if (C3) anyone wants to borrow, do not turn away. (C2)

43 "You have learned how it was said: *You* (C1) *must love your neighbor* and hate your (C3)
44 enemy.[k] •But I say this to you: love your (C3) enemies and pray for those who persecute (C2)
45 you; •in this way you will be sons of your Father in heaven, for he causes his sun to rise on bad men as well as good, and his rain to
46 fall on honest and dishonest men alike. •For if you love those who love you, what right have you to claim any credit? Even the tax
47 collectors[l] do as much, do they not? •And if you save your greetings for your brothers, are you doing anything exceptional? Even the
48 pagans do as much, do they not? •You must therefore be perfect just as your heavenly Father is perfect. (C3)

Week 1 Day 3
Four C's Meditations
on St. Matthew 5:1-48

1. Most Merciful Savior, time did not allow us to penetrate fully the great spiritual riches to be found in the scriptural passages selected for today's meditation. Nonetheless, the thoughts which did enter into our heart, with the aid of Your Holy Spirit, gave us much food for thought. In essence, we were reminded of the importance of having pure consciences and of performing acts of seed-charity.

2. In vivid contrast to the Law of the Old Testament, which was primarily concerned with external actions, You alluded to an *internal holiness* which stems from consciences being free from sin, especially fully-deliberate sins. Thus, this internal holiness would reveal itself in thoughts, words and deeds motivated by selfless love for You and for others. In the Sermon on the Mount, Lord Jesus, You taught us the necessity of having a

desire to do Your will which comes from the heart, as opposed to a merely outward conformity which is really inwardly rebellious. Consequently, when our thoughts, words and deeds are motivated by Your grace of seed-charity, a dying to selfishness occurs and we, in turn, merit increases of Your holiness, peace, joy and love.

3.   The poor in spirit of which You spoke, are those who acknowledge their sinfulness and dependency on You for every kind of good. Inspired by seed-charity, they are open to Your will and strive to accomplish it.

4.   You said, too, You will comfort Your followers who mourn, and You declared that those who strive for peace in accordance with Your will are indeed God's children and, we might add, Your adopted brothers and sisters as well. *(2)*

5.   Those who surrender themselves to You, Lord, are the salt of the earth and lights of the world. They are Your instruments for bringing genuine happiness and peace to others.

6.   You taught us that You did not come upon earth to abolish the Old Testament Law and the prophetic writings, but rather You came to complete them. *(3)* Through Your Church, which was born of Your suffering and death on the Cross, You give us the grace to fulfill the very heart of the Law and the Prophets. That is, You make it possible for us to love God first and foremost and to love our neighbor as ourselves. *(4)*

7. Thankfully, with your grace, Blessed Lord, it is now not only possible to avoid murder, for instance, but even to avoid the desire to murder which often expresses itself in anger. And now we are able to sow seeds of mercy and forgiveness towards those who offend us, rather then demanding a "eye for an eye and a tooth for a tooth." By doing so, we express Your love for them and are reminded of Your mercy and forgiveness towards us who are so unworthy to receive it.

8. Again, we fortunate Christians are able to avoid not only adultery, but even the desire to commit adultery. If we would only use Your grace, Lord, how much better our society would be! And what a blessing You have given us and our children, and the entire Church, in Your sacrament of Matrimony. In it, You have established husbands and wives in an unbreakable lifetime partnership with Yourself. May we never betray Your goodness in this regard by acts of hatred or unfaithfulness. *(For a fuller discussion of Jesus' teaching on marriage, see "The Catholic Catechism," pp. 356-362.)*

48

9.   For our many sins, forgive us, Lord, and unite the merits we earn from acts of seed-charity to Your eternal sacrifice which we participate in at Mass. It is good to know, too, that we can offer these merits to the Holy Family, so they can use them in reparation for the many offenses committed against Your Most Sacred Heart and the Immaculate Heart of Your Mother, and Your faithful guardian, St. Joseph. Amen.

Try to re-read and meditate on these Scripture passages and reflections at least one more time today.

Please read and meditate on Chapter X, Paragraphs 23 to 31 of our "Peaceful Seed Living" prayer and meditation book, Volume II.

Almsgiving in secret

1 6"Be careful not to parade your good deeds before men to attract their notice; by doing (C2) this you will lose all reward from your Father 2 in heaven. ·So when you give alms, do not have it trumpted before you; this is what the (C2) hypocrites do in the synagogues and in the (C2) streets to win men's admiration. I tell you 3 solemnly, they have had their reward. ·But when you give alms, your left hand must (C3) 4 not know what your right is doing; ·your alms-giving must be secret, and your Father who (C3) sees all that is done in secret will reward you.

Prayer in secret

5 "And when you pray, do not imitate the (C2) hypocrites: they love to say their prayers standing up in the synagogues and at the street corners for people to see them. I tell you solemnly, they have had their reward. 6 But when you pray, *go to your private room and, when you have shut your door, pray^a to* (C3) your Father who is in that secret place, and your Father who sees all that is done in secret will reward you.

How to pray. The Lord's Prayer

7 "In your prayers do not babble as the pa- (C2) gans do, for they think that by using many 8 words they will make themselves heard. ·Do not be like them; your Father knows what you (C2) 9 need before you ask him. ·So you should pray like this:

"Our Father in heaven,
may your name be held holy, (C3)
10 your kingdom come,

your will be done,
on earth as in heaven.
11 Give us today our daily bread. (C1)
12 And forgive us our debts, (C2)
as we have forgiven those who are in debt to us. (C3)
13 And do not put us to the test,
but save us from the evil one.

14 Yes, if you forgive others their failings, your (C3)
15 heavenly Father will forgive you yours; ·but
if you do not forgive others, your Father will (C2)
not forgive your failings either.

Fasting in secret

16 "When you fast do not put on a gloomy (C2)
look as the hypocrites do: they pull long faces
to let men know they are fasting. I tell you
17 solemnly, they have had their reward. ·But
when you fast, put oil on your head and wash
18 your face, ·so that no one will know you are (C3)
fasting except your Father who sees all that
is done in secret; and your Father who sees
all that is done in secret will reward you.

True treasures

19 "Do not store up treasures for yourselves (C2)
on earth, where moths and woodworms destroy them and thieves can break in and steal.
20 But store up treasures for yourselves in (C3)
heaven, where neither moth nor woodworms
destroy them and thieves cannot break in and (C2)
21 steal. ·For where your treasure is, there will
your heart be also.

The eye, the lamp of the body

22 "The lamp of the body is the eye. It follows
that if your eye is sound, your whole body
23 will be filled with light. ·But if your eye is
diseased, your whole body will be all darkness. If then, the light inside you is darkness, (C2)
what darkness that will be!

51

24   "No one can be the slave of two masters: he will either hate the first and love the sec- (C2) ond, or treat the first with respect and the second with scorn. You cannot be the slave both of God and of money.   (C2)

Trust in Providence

25   "That is why I am telling you not to worry about your life and what you are to eat, nor (C2) about your body and how you are to clothe it. Surely life means more than food, and the 26 body more than clothing! ·Look at the birds in the sky. They do not sow or reap or gather into barns; yet your heavenly Father feeds them. Are you not worth much more than 27 they are? ·Can any of you, for all his worry- (C2) ing, add one single cubit to his span of life? 28 And why worry about clothing? Think of the (C2) flowers growing in the fields; they never have 29 to work or spin; ·yet I assure you that not even Solomon in all his regalia was robed like 30 one of these. ·Now if that is how God clothes the grass in the field which is there today and thrown into the furnace tomorrow, will he

not much more look after you, you men of
31 little faith? •So do not worry; do not say, (C2)
'What are we to eat? What are we to drink? (C2)
32 How are we to be clothed?' •It is the pagans (C2)
who set their hearts on all these things. Your
heavenly Father knows you need them all. (C1)
33 Set your hearts on his kingdom first, and on
his righteousness, and all these other things (C3)
34 will be given you as well. •So do not worry (C2)
about tomorrow: tomorrow will take care of itself. Each day has enough trouble of its own.

Do not judge

1 **7** "Do not judge, and you will not be judged; (C2)
2 because the judgments you give are the
judgments you will get, and the amount you
measure out is the amount you will be given.
3 Why do you observe the splinter in your bro- (C2)
ther's eye and never notice the plank in your
4 own? •How dare you say to your brother, 'Let
me take the splinter out of your eye,' when
all the time there is a plank in your own? (C2)
5 Hypocrite! Take the plank out of your own (C2)
eye first, and then you will see clearly enough
to take the splinter out of your brother's eye.

Week 1 Day 4
Four C's Meditations
on St. Matthew 6:1-7:5

1. Heavenly Father, in today's Scripture reading, Your divine Son reveals to us the importance of good works performed in the spirit of generous, selfless charity. Our good works are to be done for Your honor and glory and for the good of others, and for our needs, as well, but certainly not for our self-glory. Moreover, when our good deeds are undertaken in the spirit of selfless seed-charity, You will also reward us. (5) And the rewards You give us always outweigh the worth of the works themselves.

2. What good work undertaken by us poor offspring of Adam and Eve would ever merit Your love and Your friendship, if it were divorced from Your love and mercy towards us, and from the merits of Your only begotten Son? What good work, however selflessly undertaken, apart from Your graciousness towards us, ever merited personal holiness and eternal life with You? None, whatsoever! Nor could the sum total of all the possible good works by themselves merit our salvation and Your love. No, Most Merciful Father, it was through the self-sacrifice of Your Son continuously throughout His life on earth, and especially when suffering and dying on the Cross, that we have access to Heaven. And it is because of His supreme act of sacrificial love that our good works merit from You ever greater increases of Your love in the

forms of sanctifying grace and the supernatural virtues and gifts. Not only that, but we
receive at the same time interior peace and
happiness. *(For a discussion of sanctifying grace and
of the supernatural virtues and gifts see "The Catholic
Catechism," pp. 193-205.)*

3.   Furthermore, Heavenly Father, as Your
Catholic Church teaches us, good works
properly performed by us can merit Your
grace for others. And this, too, is possible
only because of Your Son's unexcelled love
for mankind on the Cross of Calvary. *(In this
regard, see pp. 560-670 of "The Catholic Catechism" for
a discussion on the role of good works in gaining
indulgences for the Poor Souls in Purgatory. See also p.
125 of the "Modern Catholic Dictionary", under
"Congruous.")*

4.   Concerning good works, Heavenly
Father, Jesus taught us, "Be careful not to
parade your good deeds before men to attract
their notice; by doing this you will lose all your
reward from your Father in heaven."(6)
Instead, Jesus said good works should be
performed in secret.(7) That is, we should do
them for Your sake and for the sake of others,
and even for ourselves, but not with the
intention of seeking the approval of others
since Your approval is all that really matters,
Lord.

5.   Again, Your divine Son teaches that no
created thing can bring us lasting happiness.
That can only come from You. To make our
principal aim in life the acquisition of material
wealth, for instance, is to make wealth our

god rather than You. How foolish it is to become a slave to riches and to their pursuit. *(8)* Of course, we need money for many of the demands and desires of life, but even if these demands and desires were satisfied, we would still be unhappy, unless we also centered our lives on You and Your will. Lord, how often we have heard of the unhappy and miserable poor, but there are also the unhappy and miserable rich.

6. Jesus assures us that if we place You first in our lives, You will see that we have all we really need. *(9)* What a wonderful provider You are, Lord. Thus, to the degree we confide in You, we shall be free from worry. Yet how many of us lack this confidence as is shown by the amount of worry and anxiety in our lives. Help us, therefore, Lord, to always place our full confidence in You.

7. Jesus teaches us, too, that when we pray in the Our Father, "Give us this day our daily bread," we are to turn to You in confidence in order to have our spiritual, emotional and

material needs satisfied. *(10)* How fortunate we are to have You as our God, a God Who will never fail to help those who believe, trust and love You.

8. Lord, in the Our Father, we also pray, "Lead us not into temptation, but deliver us from (the) evil (one)." *(11)* We know we are frequently tempted to sin, including temptations from the "evil one," satan, but thankfully You have promised with each temptation to provide a way to remain in Your will. *(12)* Again, we learn the importance of placing our total trust in You. With the help of Your never-failing grace we will be able to withstand even difficult temptations and trials.

9. Finally, we noted the crucial connection You make between Your forgiveness of our sins and our forgiveness of those who offend and hurt us. *(13)* If we are to have a pure conscience, then, we must not only have a right relationship with You but a forgiving attitude towards all others as well. And when we forgive others — whether they seek our forgiveness or not — we are sowing seeds of charity and compassion, thus helping to make the world a better place in which to live.

10. Heavenly Father, in today's meditation Jesus bids us not to "judge" others so that we may not be judged by You. *(14)* This means we are not to judge their relationship with You. Even though they may indeed be outwardly sinning, even to a serious degree, You alone know fully the inner thoughts and motives of others. Therefore, You alone can perfectly

judge the degree of their guilt. *(15)* By judging others in the sense of condemning them, we are either trying to overlook our own sinfulness or trying to make our sins appear to be less serious than they are. In either case, we are bringing condemnation on ourselves. Moreover, whenever we judge others we are not helping to bring them closer to You, as we should always try to do, nor are we bringing ourselves any nearer to You. We have enough to do guarding our own consciences against sin.

11. Dear Lord, since judging others is always self-defeating, help us develop a charitable attitude towards everyone. May we always seek their salvation and rejoice in their virtues. Amen.

The more you re-read these Scriptures and meditations, the more you will get out of them.

Please read and meditate on Chapter X, Paragraphs 32 to 44 of our "Peaceful Seed Living" prayer and meditation book, Volume II.

Do not profane sacred things

6   "Do not give dogs what is holy;*a* and do (C2)
not throw your pearls in front of pigs, or they (C2)
may trample them and then turn on you and
tear you to pieces.

Effective prayer

7   "Ask, and it will be given to you; search, (C1)
and you will find; knock, and the door will (C3)
8 be opened to you. •For the one who asks (C4)
always receives; the one who searches always
finds; the one who knocks will always have
9 the door opened to him. •Is there a man
among you who would hand his son a stone (C2)
10 when he asked for bread? •Or would hand (C2)
11 him a snake when he asked for a fish? •If you,
then, who are evil, know how to give your (C2)
children what is good, how much more will
your Father in heaven give good things to (C1)
those who ask him! (C3)

The golden rule

12   "So always treat others as you would like
them to treat you; that is the meaning of the (C3)
Law and the Prophets.

The two ways

13   "Enter by the narrow gate, since the road (C1)
that leads to perdition is wide and spacious, (C2)
14 and many take it; •but it is a narrow gate and (C3)
a hard road that leads to life, and only a few (C4)
find it.

False prophets

15   "Beware of false prophets*b* who come to (C2)
you disguised as sheep but underneath are
16 ravenous wolves. •You will be able to tell (C2)

59

them by their fruits. Can people pick grapes
17 from thorns, or figs from thistles? ·In the
same way, a sound tree produces good fruit (C3)
18 but a rotten tree bad fruit. ·A sound tree (C2)
cannot bear bad fruit, nor a rotten tree bear (C2)
19 good fruit. ·Any tree that does not produce (C2)
good fruit is cut down and thrown on the fire.
20 I repeat, you will be able to tell them by their
fruits.

The true disciple

21   "It is not those who say to me, 'Lord, (C1)
Lord,' who will enter the kingdom of heaven,
but the person who does the will of my Fa- (C3)
22 ther in heaven. ·When the day^c comes many
will say to me, 'Lord, Lord, did we not (C2)
prophesy in your name, cast out demons in
your name, work many miracles in your
23 name?' ·Then I shall tell them to their faces:
I have never known you; *away from me, you* (C2)
evil men!

24   "Therefore, everyone who listens to these
words of mine and acts on them will be like (C3)
a sensible man who built his house on rock.
25 Rain came down, floods rose, gales blew and
hurled themselves against that house, and it
26 did not fall: it was founded on rock. ·But
everyone who listens to these words of mine
and does not act on them will be like a stupid (C2)

27 man who built his house on sand. •Rain came
down, floods rose, gales blew and struck that
house, and it fell; and what a fall it had!"

The amazement of the crowds

28 Jesus had now finished what he wanted to
say, and his teaching made a deep impression
29 on the people •because he taught them with
authority, and not like their own scribes.*d*

III. THE KINGDOM OF HEAVEN IS PREACHED

A. NARRATIVE SECTION: TEN MIRACLES

Cure of a leper

1 **8** After he had come down from the moun-
2 tain large crowds followed him. •A leper
now came up and bowed low in front of him.
"Sir," he said, "if you want to, you can cure (C1)
3 me." •Jesus stretched out his hand, touched
him and said, "Of course I want to! Be
cured!" And his leprosy was cured at once. (C3)
4 Then Jesus said to him, "Mind you do not
tell anyone, but go and show yourself to the
priest and make the offering prescribed by
Moses, as evidence for them."

61

5   When he went into Capernaum a centurion
6 came up and pleaded with him. •"Sir," he said
"my servant is lying at home paralyzed, and (C3)
7 in great pain." •"I will come myself and cure (C3)
8 him," said Jesus. •The centurion replied,
"Sir, I am not worthy to have you under my (C2)
roof; just give the word and my servant will
9 be cured. •For I am under authority myself, (C1)
and have soldiers under me; and I say to one
man: Go, and he goes; to another: Come
here, and he comes; to my servant: Do this,
10 and he does it." •When Jesus heard this he
was astonished and said to those following
him, "I tell you solemnly, nowhere in Israel
11 have I found faith like this. •And I tell you (C1)
that many will come from east and west to
take their places with Abraham and Isaac and
Jacob at the feast in the kingdom of heaven; (C3)
12 but the subjects of the kingdom*a* will be (C2)
turned out into the dark, where there will be
13 weeping and grinding of teeth." •And to the
centurion Jesus said, "Go back, then; you
have believed, so let this be done for you." (C1)
And the servant was cured at that moment. (C3)

Cure of Peter's mother-in-law

14   And going into Peter's house Jesus found
15 Peter's mother-in-law in bed with fever. •He
touched her hand and the fever left her, and (C3)
she got up and began to wait on him.

A number of cures

16   That evening they brought him many who
were possessed by devils. He cast out the
spirits with a word and cured all who were (C3)
17 sick. •This was to fulfill the prophecy of
Isaiah:

He took our sicknesses away and carried our
*   diseases, for us.*b

18 When Jesus saw the great crowds all about
him he gave orders to leave for the other
19 side.[c] •One of the scribes then came up and
said to him, "Master, I will follow you wher-
20 ever you go." •Jesus replied, "Foxes have (C3)
holes and the birds of the air have nests, but
the Son of Man has nowhere to lay his head."
21 Another man, one of his disciples, said to
him, "Sir, let me go and bury my father first."
22 But Jesus replied, "Follow me, and leave the
dead to bury their dead."

The calming of the storm

23 Then he got into the boat followed by his
24 disciples. •Without warning a storm broke
over the lake, so violent that the waves were
breaking right over the boat. But he was
25 asleep. •So they went to him and woke him
saying, "Save us, Lord, we are going down!" (C1)
26 And he said to them, "Why are you so frightened, you men of little faith?" And with that (C1)
he stood up and rebuked the winds and the (C2)
27 sea; and all was calm again. •The men were astounded and said, "Whatever kind of man is
this? Even the winds and the sea obey him."

The demoniacs of Gadara

28 When he reached the country of the Gada-
renes on the other side, two demoniacs came
toward him out of the tombs—creatures so
29 fierce that no one could pass that way. •They
stood there shouting, "What do you want
with us, Son of God? Have you come here
30 to torture us before the time?"[d] •Now some
distance away there was a large herd of pigs
31 feeding, •and the devils pleaded with Jesus,
"If you cast us out, send us into the herd of
32 pigs." •And he said to them, "Go then," and
they came out and made for the pigs; and at
that the whole herd charged down the cliff
33 into the lake and perished in the water. •The

63

swineherds ran off and made for the town,
where they told the whole story, including
34 what had happened to the demoniacs. •At this
the whole town set out to meet Jesus; and as
soon as they saw him they implored him to
leave the neighborhood.

Week 1 Day 5
Four C's Meditations
on St. Matthew 7:6-8:34

1.   Jesus, Our Lord and Our God, in today's
Scripture reading You teach us the
importance of praying persistently. Thus You
said, "Ask and it will be given to you; search
and you will find, knock and the door will be
opened to you."(16) Yet, we must admit that,
at times, we find it hard to believe You and
the Father will provide us with all our needs
and see us through every difficulty. This is
especially true when things are not going well
for us and it seems as if our prayers are not
being answered. But we must learn to be
patient as You do not always respond to us in
ways we can understand. Nor do You always
answer us as quickly as we would like.(17)

Lord, help us to realize this when we are impatient or begin to doubt Your promise to take care of our every need. Increase our faith in You and inspire us to keep on "knocking." Surely, You will answer our prayers, and in a manner that is best for us and for others.

2.   Next, Merciful Lord, Matthew recounts for us Your Golden Rule, "Always treat others as you would like them to treat you."(18) Obviously, we want to be treated justly and with charity. Therefore, help us always to do the same to others. And among those who most need our charity are the Poor Souls in Purgatory, since they cannot help themselves. May we never forget them. *(See Chapter XII, Volume II of "Peaceful Seed Living" for information on obtaining indulgences for the Poor Souls in Purgatory. And for a discussion of Purgatory itself see pp. 273-280 in "The Catholic Catechism.")*

3.   Most Sacred Heart of Jesus, You died so everyone might receive salvation.(19) Yet, You also tell us the way to salvation is not easy and that many take the path which leads to eternal damnation.

4.   "Enter by the narrow gate, since the road that leads to perdition is wide and spacious, and many take it; but it is only a narrow gate and a hard road that leads to life, and only a few find it."(20)

5.   These are thought-provoking words, Lord. Thankfully, You will always supply us with the graces we need to prepare ourselves for Heaven, but we must pray for them and

work very hard to use them properly. And if we should fall away from You through our sins, we must not hesitate to repent and return to the comfort of Your Sacred Heart.

6. Blessed Lord, in today's meditation You warn us against false prophets who appear to be genuine but "underneath are ravenous wolves."(21) While on the surface they appear to be Your true messengers, on closer observation their true colors can be recognized by their words which fail to reflect the teaching of Your Catholic Church. We have in mind, especially, those who for one reason or another remain outwardly Catholics but in fact, "bite the hands" of those who feed them. That is, they bite the hands of the Pope and the bishops who are in union with him as their head. *(For information on the infallibility of the Pope and bishops in union with him, read pp. 227-233 of "The Catholic Catechism.")*

7. Lord, in today's reading, our attention focused on the fact You said it is not those who only cry out, "Lord, Lord," who enter

Your Kingdom, but those who actually do the will of Your Father. *(22)* Thus, if we outwardly say and do what we should, this is pleasing to You, but it is not enough. What mainly counts is the underlying spirit with which we speak and act. What is this underlying spirit? It is our love for You shown by our avoidance of sin, especially mortal sin. Thus, if we have the stain of a grave sin on our souls, we are not in Your friendship and our salvation is in jeopardy. We need, then, not only faith and trust in You, but also a conscience free from serious sins so our words and deeds will be motivated by sacrificial seed-charity, the one grace that guarantees we are in Your friendship and in the state of grace. *(23)* *(For a discussion on the nature of mortal sin, see pp. 293-295 of "The Catholic Catechism.")*

8.   Most Loving and Merciful Jesus, in Your description of the wise man who built his house on rock, You taught us the great value of the gift of constancy.

9.   "Therefore, everyone who listens to these words of mine and acts on them will be like a sensible man who built his house on rock. Rain come down, floods rose, gales blew and hurled themselves against that house, and it did not fall: it was founded on rock. But everyone who listens to these words of mine and does not act on them will be like a stupid man who built his house on sand. Rain came down, floods rose, gales blew and struck that house, and it fell; and what a fall it had!" *(24)*

10. We learn from this that when we constantly exercise seed-charity, and also faith on which seed-charity must be built, we are able to withstand the onslaughts of the world, the flesh and the devil. Equally important is the fact that we also grow in sanctity and obtain that interior peace which the world cannot give.(25) Therefore, Lord, inspire us every day to seek the gift of constancy so we may remain in Your friendship and have a foretaste of eternal life.

11. In chapter eight, Jesus, when You spoke of the faith of the leper and the centurion, You implied that faith in You was essential in order to benefit from Your love. And the faith of the centurion was particularly remarkable since he was not a Jew looking for the long-promised Savior of mankind.

12. "After he had come down from the mountain large crowds followed him. A leper came up and bowed low in front if him. 'Sir,' he said, 'if you want to, you can cure me.'

Jesus stretched out his hand, touched him and said, 'Of course I want to! Be cured!' And his leprosy was cured at once . . ." "When he went into Capernaum a centurion came up and pleaded with him. 'Sir,' he said 'my servant is lying at home paralyzed, and in great pain.' 'I will come myself and cure him,' said Jesus. The centurion replied, 'Sir, I am not worthy to have you under my roof; just give the word and my servant will be cured. For I am under authority myself, and have soldiers under me; and I say to one man: Go, and he goes; to another: Come here, and he comes; to my servant: Do this, and he does it.' When Jesus heard this he was astonished and said to those following him, 'I tell you solemnly, nowhere in Israel have I found faith like this. And I tell you that many will come from east and west to take their places with Abraham and Isaac and Jacob at the feast in the kingdom of heaven; but the subjects of the kingdom will be turned out into the dark, where there will be weeping and grinding of teeth.' And to the centurion Jesus said, 'Go back, then; you have believed, so let this be done for you.' And the servant was cured at that moment."(26)

13. Lord, You also referred to the super-natural virtue of faith in that well-known account of the disciples who were terrified by a lake storm. Believing they would perish in their boat, they cried out to You for help, but You rebuked them for having so little faith (belief) in You.

69

14. "Then he got into the boat followed by his disciples. Without warning a storm broke over the lake, so violent that the waves were breaking right over the boat. But he was asleep. So they went to him and woke him saying, 'Save us, Lord, we are going down!' And he said to them, 'Why are you so frightened, you men of little faith?' And with that he stood up and rebuked the wind and the sea; and all was calm again. The men were astounded and said, 'Whatever kind of man is this? Even the winds and the sea obey him.'"(27)

15. Lord, there are many of us, today, who are so much like Your disciples were at that moment. Thus, as we noted in yesterday's meditation, when troubles come, especially major ones, we often behave as if we have little or no faith in Your promise to take care of us.(28) We often fall apart emotionally, and we fail to really believe You care for us and

want to take full charge of our lives. Therefore, increase our confidence (faith, trust) in You, so when the inevitable storms of life occur, we will remain calm knowing You will never desert us and will see us through them safely, as long· as we remain Your friends.

16.   Jesus, Mary, Joseph! Holy Family, pray for us! Amen.

The more you re-read these Scriptures and meditations, the more you will get out of them.

Please refer to Chapter X, Paragraphs 45 to 54 of our "Peaceful Seed Living" prayer and meditation book, Volume II.

WEEK 1 DAY 6
The Gospel of St. Matthew
Chapter 9:1-38

Cure of a paralytic

9 ¹He got back in the boat, crossed the water ²and came to his own town.*a* •Then some people appeared, bringing him a paralytic (C3) stretched out on a bed. Seeing their faith, (C1) Jesus said to the paralytic, "Courage, my ³child, your sins are forgiven." •And at this (C3) some scribes said to themselves, "This man ⁴is blaspheming." •Knowing what was in their (C2) minds Jesus said, "Why do you have such (C2) ⁵wicked thoughts in your hearts? •Now, which of these is easier: to say, 'Your sins are for-⁶given,' or to say, 'Get up and walk?' •But to prove to you that the Son of Man has au-thority on earth to forgive sins,"—he said to the paralytic—"get up, and pick up your bed (C3) ⁷and go off home." •And the man got up and ⁸went home. •A feeling of awe came over the crowd when they saw this, and they praised God for giving such power to men. (C3)

The call of Matthew

⁹ As Jesus was walking on from there he saw a man named Matthew*b* sitting by the cus- (C1) toms house, and he said to him, "Follow (C3) me." And he got up and followed him.

Eating with sinners

¹⁰ While he was at dinner in the house it hap-pened that a number of tax collectors and sinners*c* came to sit at the table with Jesus and (C2) ¹¹his disciples. •When the Pharisees saw this, they said to his disciples, "Why does your master eat with tax collectors and sinners?" (C2) ¹²When he heard this he replied, "It is not the ¹³healthy who need the doctor, but the sick. •Go

72

and learn the meaning of the words: *What I want is mercy, not sacrifice.*^d And indeed I did (C3) not come to call the virtuous, but sinners." (C2)

A discussion on fasting

14 Then John's^e disciples came to him and said, "Why is it that we and the Pharisees
15 fast, but your disciples do not?" •Jesus re- (C3) plied, "Surely the bridegroom's attendants would never think of mourning as long as the (C2) bridegroom is still with them? But the time will come for the bridegroom to be taken
16 away from them, and then they will fast. •No (C3) one puts a piece of unshrunken cloth on to an old cloak, because the patch pulls away from the cloak and the tear gets worse.
17 Nor do people put new wine into old wine-skins; if they do, the skins burst, the wine runs out, and the skins are lost. No; they put new wine into fresh skins and both are pre-served."^f

Cure of the woman with a hemorrhage. The official's daughter raised to life

18 While he was speaking to them, up came one of the officials, who bowed low in front of him and said, "My daughter has just died, but come and lay your hand on her and her (C1)
19 life will be saved." •Jesus rose and, with his (C3) disciples, followed him.
20 Then from behind him came a woman, who had suffered from a hemorrhage for twelve years, and she touched the fringe of
21 his cloak, •for she said to herself, "If I can only touch his cloak I shall be well again." (C1)
22 Jesus turned round and saw her; and he said to her, "Courage, my daughter, your faith has restored you to health." And from that mo- (C1) ment the woman was well again. (C3)
23 When Jesus reached the official's house and saw the flute-players, with the crowd
24 making a commotion^g he said, •"Get out of

73

here; the little girl is not dead, she is asleep."
25 And they laughed at him. •But when the people had been turned out he went inside and took the little girl by the hand; and she stood
26 up. •And the news spread all round the (C 3) countryside.

Cure of two blind men

27 As Jesus went on his way two blind men followed him shouting, "Take pity on us, Son
28 of David." •And when Jesus reached the (C1) house the blind men came up with him and he said to them, "Do you believe I can do
29 this?" They said, "Sir, we do." •Then he (C1) touched their eyes saying, "Your faith de-
30 serves it, so let this be done for you." •And (C1) their sight returned. Then Jesus sternly warned them, "Take care that no one learns
31 about this." •But when they had gone, they talked about him all over the countryside. (C2)

Cure of a dumb demoniac

32 They had only just left when a man was
33 brought to him, a dumb demoniac. •And when the devil was cast out, the dumb man (C3) spoke and the people were amazed. "Nothing like this has ever been seen in Israel" they

34 said. •But the Pharisees said, "It is through
the prince of devils tha* he casts out devils." (C3)

The distress of the crowds

35 Jesus made a tour through all the towns
and villages, teaching in their synagogues,
proclaiming the Good News of the kingdom (C3)
and curing all kinds of diseases and sickness.
36 And when he saw the crowds he felt sorry
for them because they were harassed and de- (C3)
37 jected, like sheep without a shepherd. •Then
he said to his disciples, "The harvest is rich
38 but the laborers are few, •so ask the Lord of (C1)
the harvest to send laborers to his harvest." (C3)

Week 1 Day 6
Four C's Meditations
on St. Matthew 9:1-38

1. Jesus, in this meditation, we were
reminded of Your loving response to those
who turn to You with faith for healing, either
for themselves or for others. For instance, in
the case of the woman who had hemor-
rhaged for twelve years, it was her own faith
in You which occasioned the generous
outpouring of Your Sacred Heart.(29) Again,

with respect to the two blind men, it was their own faith in You that was the means for receiving Your healing power. *(30)* And in yesterday's meditation, it was the centurion's faith which was the vehicle for the healing of his servant. *(31)*

2. Actually, dear Jesus, You respond favorably to heal all who turn to You with faith, trust and seed-charity. This is always the case with respect to spiritual illnesses, i.e., sinful afflictions, which are often the bases for psychological maladies. You also, on occasion, miraculously heal our physical illnesses. Lord, may we never lose our belief and trust in You, Who are our true Friend as well as our divine Savior. Others, even those closest to us, may desert us, but You never will as long as we remain Your friends. *(For information on the healing effects of the sacrament of Anointing, see "The Catholic Catechism" pp. 240-243.)*

3. We noticed also, Lord, in today's reading that those who had no faith in You did not receive the tenderness of Your love. These included the scribes who claimed You were blaspheming, and the Pharisees who said You were an agent of the devil. *(32)* They, of course, were not open to Your love, having hardened hearts. So it was not that You did not love them, but rather they did not love You. And clearly their lack of faith prevented it.

4. It would certainly seem that the Pharisees, in this particular instance, harbored evil consciences. Calling You an

agent of satan, they refused to acknowledge the obvious. That is, only someone in God's friendship could cast out a demon, as You did in the case of the dumb demoniac.(33) Yet, Lord, even those whose consciences were defiled with sins were the objects of Your mercy and charity since You said to the Pharisees themselves: "And indeed, I did not come to call the virtuous (to repentance) but sinners."(34) Their great problem, however, was that as a group they did not believe they were sinners. Consequently, they were unable to be reconciled to You and to the Father.

5.   Jesus, when the crowd witnessed Your healing of the paralytic and Your forgiveness of his sins, they, unlike the Pharisees, acknowledged that You were sent from God. Moreover, they reflected their charity for God when they praised the Father because of You. "And they praised God for giving such power

77

to men."*(35)* And those who brought the paralytic to You to be cured, not only revealed their faith in You but manifested their charity for the paralytic as well. The disciples of John the Baptist also reflected their love for You when they rejoiced at being in Your presence.*(36)*

6. Lord, unlike Your disciples and friends who were with You while You were on earth, we cannot see You in the flesh. But we can encounter You in a special way when we are in Your Eucharistic Presence. May such moments always be occasions of rejoicing and growth in our charity towards You. What is more, as we learn to love You increasingly, we will be better able to sacrifice ourselves for others. *(For more on the Eucharistic presence see pp. 479-481 of "The Catholic Catechism.")*

7. Among those who need our sacrificial love, may we never forget the Poor Souls in Purgatory who are unable to help themselves. And in their charity, may they never forget us in our needs. *(For an informative discussion on Purgatory and the Poor Souls inhabiting there, read "The Catholic Catechism," pp-273-280.)*

8. Jesus, You persisted in the exercise of sacrificial love (seed-charity) until Your final gasps on the Cross of Calvary, therefore meriting eternal life for us. Grant that we also may persevere in sacrificial love until we die, no matter how difficult the ordeals we may encounter, so the everlasting joys You have gained for us may never be lost. As a very effective means of promoting this goal, inspire

us to reflect often on the many sufferings You endured for us, especially during the final days of Your earthly life.

9. Jesus, Our Lord, we adore You, help us to love You more and more. Amen.

Please re-read these Scriptures for the day and ask the Holy Spirit to help you draw more insights which you can apply to your daily life.

Also refer to Chapter X, Paragraphs 55 to 71 of our "Peaceful Seed Living" prayer and meditation book, Volume II.

B. THE INSTRUCTION OF THE APOSTLES

The mission of the Twelve

1 **10** He summoned his twelve disciples, and gave them authority over unclean spir- (C2) its with power to cast them out and to cure all kinds of diseases and sickness.

2 These are the names of the twelve apostles: first, Simon who is called Peter, and his brother Andrew; James the son of Zebedee,
3 and his brother John; ·Philip and Bartholomew; Thomas, and Matthew the tax collector; James the son of Alphaeus, and Thad-
4 daeus; ·Simon the Zealot and Judas Iscariot,
5 the one who was to betray him. ·These twelve Jesus sent out, instructing them as follows:

"Do not turn your steps to pagan territory,
6 and do not enter any Samaritan town; ·go rather to the lost sheep of the House of Is- (C2)
7 rael. ·And as you go, proclaim that the king- (C3)
8 dom of heaven is close at hand. ·Cure the (C3) sick, raise the dead, cleanse the lepers, cast (C2) out devils. You received without charge, give (C3)
9 without charge. ·Provide yourselves with no gold or silver, not even with a few coppers
10 for your purses, ·with no haversack for the journey or spare tunic or footwear or a staff, for the workman deserves his keep.

11 "Whatever town or village you go into, ask for someone trustworthy and stay with him
12 until you leave. ·As you enter his house, sa- (C3)
13 lute it, ·and if the house deserves it, let your peace descend upon it; if it does not, let your (C3)
14 peace come back to you. ·And if anyone does not welcome you or listen to what you have (C2) to say, as you walk out of the house or town
15 shake the dust from your feet. ·I tell you

solemnly, on the day of Judgment it will not (C2)
go as hard with the land of Sodom and
16 Gomorrah as with that town. •Remember, I (C2)
am sending you out like sheep among wolves; (C2)
so be cunning as serpents and yet as harmless (C2)
as doves.

The missionaries will be persecuted[a]

17   "Beware of men: they will hand you over
to sanhedrins and scourge you in their syna-
18 gogues. •You will be dragged before gover- (C2)
nors and kings for my sake, to bear witness (C1)
19 before them and the pagans. •But when they (C3)
hand you over, do not worry about how to
speak or what to say; what you are to say will
20 be given to you when the time comes; •be-
cause it is not you who will be speaking; the
Spirit of your Father will be speaking in you.
21   "Brother will betray brother to death, and (C2)
the father his child; children will rise against
their parents and have them put to death. (C2)
22 You will be hated by all men on account of
my name; but the man who stands firm to the (C2)
23 end will be saved. •If they persecute you in (C4)
one town, take refuge in the next; and if they (C2)
persecute you in that, take refuge in another. (C2)
I tell you solemnly, you will not have gone
the round of the towns of Israel before the
Son of Man comes.
24   "The disciple is not superior to his teacher,
25 nor the slave to his master. •It is enough for (C3)
the disciple that he should grow to be like
his teacher, and the slave like his master. If
they have called the master of the house (C2)
Beelzebul, what will they not say of his
household?

Open and fearless speech

26   "Do not be afraid of them therefore. For (C1)
everything that is now covered will be uncov-
ered, and everything now hidden will be
27 made clear. •What I say to you in the dark,

81

tell in the daylight; what you hear in whispers, (C3)
proclaim from the housetops.

28 "Do not be afraid of those who kill the (C1) (C2)
body but cannot kill the soul; fear him rather
who can destroy both body and soul in hell. (C2)

29 Can you not buy two sparrows for a penny?
And yet not one falls to the ground without

30 your Father knowing. •Why, every hair on

31 your head has been counted. •So there is no
need to be afraid; you are worth more than
hundreds of sparrows.

32 "So if anyone declares himself for me in
the presence of men, I will declare myself for (C3)
him in the presence of my Father in heaven.

33 But the one who disowns me in the presence (C2)
of men, I will disown in the presence of my
Father in heaven.

Jesus, the cause of dissension

34 "Do not suppose that I have come to bring
peace to the earth: it is not peace I have come

35 to bring, but a sword. •For I have come to
set *a man against his father, a daughter
against her mother, a daughter-in-law against*

36 *her mother-in-law. •A man's enemies will be* (C2)
those of his own household.[b]

37 "Any one who prefers father or mother to (C2)
me is not worthy of me. Anyone who prefers (C2)
son or daughter to me is not worthy of me.

38 Anyone who does not take his cross and fol- (C2)
low in my footsteps is not worthy of me.

39 Anyone who finds his life will lose it; anyone (C2)
who loses his life for my sake will find it. (C3)

Conclusion

40 "Anyone who welcomes you welcomes (C3)
me; and those who welcome me welcome the (C3)
one who sent me.

41 "Anyone who welcomes a prophet be- (C3)
cause he is a prophet will have a prophet's
reward; and anyone who welcomes a holy (C3)
man because he is a holy man will have a holy (C2)
man's reward.

42 "If anyone gives so much as a cup of cold
water to one of these little ones because he (C3)
is a disciple, then I tell you solemnly, he will
most certainly not lose his reward."

Week 1 Day 7
Four C's Meditations
on St. Matthew 10:1-42

1.   In today's reading, Jesus, we noted You commissioned the twelve Apostles to proclaim the Gospel or Good News of Your messianic Kingdom. To announce the Gospel, as they did, with the intention of seeking converts to Your Church or Kingdom is truly an act of sacrificial love. And those who become converts reap the benefits of Your sacrificial death and glorious Resurrection. Upon Baptism, they become members of Your Kingdom and share in Your divine nature. *(37)* What is more, they are given graces enabling them to become saints. *(See "The Catholic Catechism," for information on the nature of this kingdom, pp. 208-209, and read pp 505-513 for a detailed presentation on the nature of Baptism.)*

2.   Lord, all who are Christians — not simply the clergy and Religious — are called to evangelize or proclaim the Gospel of the Kingdom of Heaven to others. Therefore, help us to be effective signs and instruments of Your Kingdom, not only by proclaiming the Gospel clearly and without error, but also by our example of holy living. May it never be said of us that some sin of ours contributed to the exclusion of someone else from Your Kingdom. To this end, help us to be especially charitable to members of our families, encouraging them to remain as Your friends, and to be fervent witnesses of Your saving Gospel. *(The duty of the laity to evangelize is*

underscored by the Second Vatican Council. See p. 437 of "The Catholic Catechism.")

3. Jesus, Mary, Joseph! Have mercy on us who are often poor reflections of Your love among the members of our families and in our neighborhoods and communities.

4. We also observed in today's meditation, Lord, that You tested Your Apostles' belief and trust in You by sending them to evangelize with what would appear to be no material provisions. *(38)* This reminded us of Your earlier teaching in chapter six where You promised that those who placed God and His Kingdom first in their lives would receive all things necessary to live in accordance with His will.

5. "So do not worry, do not say, what are we to eat? What are we to drink? How are we to be clothed?... It is the pagans who set their hearts on all these things. Your heavenly Father knows that you need them all. Set

your hearts on his kingdom first, on his righteousness, and all these other things will be given to you as well."*(39)*

6.   Jesus, Savior, in preparing the Apostles for their journey, You instructed them not to bless those who refused to receive them and the Gospel.*(40)* In light of this, grant that the laity might always honor Your apostolic ministers, who are loyal to the Holy Father, the Pope. May the many blessings they can confer, as Your special representatives, be readily sought. *(For further information on the apostolic ministry of bishops, priests and deacons, read pp. 520-531 of "The Catholic Catechism.")*

7.   Lord, You revealed the sufferings Your Apostles would have to endure as the price of faithful service. You said they would be beaten by religious authorities and they would be betrayed, hated and persecuted.*(41)* At first glance this does not seem fair and indeed it is not. But it was not You Who would cause this evil, but those who hated You and Your Gospel.

8.   You rightly pointed out to Your Apostles, they must not expect to be treated any more leniently than You were treated at the hands of Your enemies.*(42)* Elsewhere You said, "If anyone wants to be a follower of mine, let him renounce himself and take up his cross and follow me."*(43)* And Your servants, Sts. Paul and Barnabas stated, "We all have to experience many hardships before we enter the kingdom of God."*(44)*

9. Despite their sufferings on account of Your Name, Your followers must persist in being faithful to You and Your will. But You also promised they would be greatly rewarded for doing so. "Happy are you when people abuse you and persecute you and speak all kinds of calumny against you on my account. Rejoice and be glad, for your reward will be great in heaven; this is how they persecuted the prophets before you."*(45)*

10. In Your own case, Lord, Your excruciating suffering on earth was followed by the glory of Your bodily Resurrection from the dead, Your bodily Ascension into Heaven and the opening of the gates of Your heavenly Kingdom to all who would follow in Your footsteps.

11. We then, who suffer for Your Name's sake by continually combating the sins of the world, the flesh and the devil will draw ever closer to You. And if we remain constant until the end, we will have merited through You eternal life in Your heavenly Kingdom. Moreover, our sufferings undertaken as Your followers can merit graces for others. *(For more on this, see Volume I of "Peaceful Seed Living," Chapter IV, Paragraphs 1 to 5.)*

12. Another thing You taught us, Jesus, is that we must not be afraid to proclaim You and Your Good News to others, even if it means our death, since You and Your Father will always strengthen and guide us.*(46)*

Nevertheless, there are times when some of us actually feel afraid or even ashamed to share You and Your Gospel with others. Consequently, help us to overcome our fears and sinful shame, and may all we do be pleasing in Your sight. Amen.

Try to read these Scripture passages and meditations several times a day in a reflective manner. Each time you do so, the Holy Spirit will give you more insights.

Now reflectively read Chapter X, Paragraphs 72 to 78 of our "Peaceful Seed Living," prayer and meditation book, Volume II.

IV. THE MYSTERY
OF THE KINGDOM
OF HEAVEN

A. NARRATIVE SECTION

1 **11** When Jesus had finished instructing his (C3) twelve disciples he moved on from there to teach and preach in their towns.*a*

The Baptist's question. Jesus commends him

2 Now John in his prison had heard what Christ was doing and he sent his disciples to
3 ask him, ·"Are you the one who is to come, or have we got to wait for someone else?"
4 Jesus answered, "Go back and tell John what
5 you hear and see; ·the blind see again, and (C3) the lame walk, lepers are cleansed, and the (C3) deaf hear, and the dead are raised to life and (C3) the Good News is proclaimed to the poor;*b* (C3)
6 and happy is the man who does not lose faith (C1) in me." (C2)

7 As the messengers were leaving, Jesus began to talk to the people about John: "What did you go out into the wilderness to see? A
8 reed swaying in the breeze? No? ·Then what did you go out to see? A man wearing fine clothes? Oh no, those who wear fine clothes
9 are to be found in palaces. ·Then what did you go out for? To see a prophet? Yes, I tell
10 you, and much more than a prophet: ·he is the one of whom scripture says:

Look, I am going to send my messenger
    before you;
*he will prepare your way before you.*c   (C3)

89

11 "I tell you solemnly, of all the children born of women, a greater than John the Baptist has never been seen; yet the least in the kingdom of heaven is greater than he is. (C3)

12 Since John the Baptist came, up to this present time, the kingdom of heaven has been subjected to violence and the violent are tak- (C2)
13 ing it by storm. •Because it was toward John that all the prophecies of the prophets and of
14 the Law were leading; •and he, if you will (C1) believe me, is the Elijah who was to re-
15 turn.*d* •If anyone has ears to hear, let him listen!

Jesus condemns his contemporaries

16 "What description can I find for this generation? It is like children shouting to each other as they sit in the market place:

17   'We played the pipes for you,
    and you wouldn't dance; (C2)
    we sang dirges,
    and you wouldn't be mourners.' (C2)

18 "For John came, neither eating nor drink-
19 ing, and they say, 'He is possessed.' •The (C2) Son of Man came, eating and drinking, and they say, 'Look, a glutton and a drunkard, a (C2) friend of tax collectors and sinners.' Yet wisdom has been proved right by her ac- (C3) tions."

20 Then he began to reproach the towns in which most of his miracles had been worked, because they refused to repent. (C2)

21 "Alas for you, Chorazin! Alas for you, (C2) Bethsaida! For if the miracles done in you had been done in Tyre and Sidon, they (C3) would have repented long ago in sack-
22 cloth and ashes. ·And still, I tell you that it will not go as hard on Judgment day with
23 Tyre and Sidon as with you. ·And as for you, Capernaum, did you want to be exalted as high as heaven? *You shall be thrown down to hell.*ᵉ For if the miracles done in you (C2) had been done in Sodom, it would
24 have been standing yet. ·And still, I tell you that it will not go as hard with the land of Sodom on Judgment day as with (C2) you."

The Good News revealed to the simple. The Father and the Son

25 At that time Jesus exclaimed, "I bless you, Father, Lord of heaven and of earth, for hiding these things from the learned and the (C2) clever and revealing them to mere children. (C1)
26 Yes, Father, for that is what it pleased you
27 to do. ·Everything has been entrusted to me by my Father; and no one knows the Son except the Father, just as no one knows the Father except the Son and those to whom the Son chooses to reveal him.

The gentle mastery of Christ

28 "Come to me, all you who labor and are overburdened, and I will give you rest.
29 Shoulder my yoke and learn from me, for I (C3) am gentle and humble in heart, *and you will* (C1)
30 *find rest for your souls*ᶠ·Yes, my yoke is easy and my burden light."

91

1 **12** At that time Jesus took a walk one sabbath day through the cornfields. His disciples were hungry and began to pick ears 2 of corn and eat them. •The Pharisees noticed it and said to him, "Look, your disciples are doing something that is forbidden on the sab-3 bath." •But he said to them, "Have you not read what David did when he and his follow-4 ers were hungry—•how he went into the house of God and how they ate the loaves of offering which neither he nor his followers were allowed to eat, but which were for the 5 priests alone? •Or again, have you not read in the Law that on the sabbath day the Temple priests break the sabbath without being 6 blamed for it? •Now here, I tell you, is some-7 thing greater than the Temple. •And if you had understood the meaning of the words: *What I want is mercy, not sacrifice,* you (C3) would not have condemned the blameless. 8 For the Son of Man is master of the sabbath."

9 He moved on from there and went to their
10 synagogue, •and a man was there at the time
who had a withered hand. They asked him,
"Is it against the law to cure a man on the
sabbath day?" hoping for something to use (C2)
11 against him. •But he said to them, "If any one
of you here had only one sheep and it fell
down a hole on the sabbath day, would he not
12 get hold of it and lift it out? •Now a man is
far more important than a sheep, so it follows
that it is permitted to do good on the sabbath (C3)
13 day." •Then he said to the man, "Stretch out (C3)
your hand." He stretched it out and his hand
14 was better, as sound as the other one. •At
this the Pharisees went out and began to
plot against him, discussing how to destroy (C2)
him.

Jesus the "servant of Yahweh"

15 Jesus knew this and withdrew from the
district. Many followed him and he cured (C3)
16 them all, •but warned them not to make him
17 known. •This was to fulfill the prophecy of
Isaiah:

18 *Here is my servant whom I have chosen,*
my beloved, the favorite of my soul.
I will endow him with my spirit,
and he will proclaim the true faith to the na-
tions.
19 *He will not brawl or shout,*
nor will anyone hear his voice in the streets.
20 *He will not break the crushed reed,*
nor put out the smouldering wick
till he has led the truth to victory:
21 *in his name the nations will put their hope.*[a]

Jesus and Beelzebul

22 Then they brought to him a blind and
dumb demoniac; and he cured him, so that (C3)
23 the dumb man could speak and see. •All the

93

people were astounded and said, "Can this
24 be the Son of David?" ·But when the Pharisees heard this they said, "The man casts out (C2)
devils only through Beelzebul,[b] the prince of
devils."

25 Knowing what was in their minds he said
to them, "Every kingdom divided against it- (C2)
self is heading for ruin; and no town, no
household divided against itself can stand. (C2)
26 Now if Satan casts out Satan, he is divided
against himself; so how can his kingdom
27 stand? ·And if it is through Beelzebul that I
cast out devils, through whom do your own (C2)
experts cast them out? Let them be your
28 judges, then. ·But if it is through the Spirit
of God that I cast devils out, then know that
the kingdom of God has overtaken you.

29 "Or again, how can anyone make his way
into a strong man's house and burgle his
property unless he has tied up the strong man (C2)
first? Only then can he burgle his house.

30 "He who is not with me is against me, and (C2)
he who does not gather with me scatters.
31 And so I tell you, every one of men's sins (C2)
and blasphemies will be forgiven, but blasphemy against the Spirit will not be forgiven. (C2)
32 And anyone who says a word against the (C2)
Son of Man will be forgiven; but let anyone
speak against the Holy Spirit and he will not (C2)
be forgiven either in this world or in the next.

Week 2 Day 1
Four C's Meditations
on St. Matthew 11:1-12:32

1. Today, Most Gracious Savior, we observed in our Scripture reading, that even the disciples of Your cousin, John the Baptist, nursed some doubts about Your messiahship. You, of course, assured them You were indeed the long-expected Savior of the world. But You also added, "Happy is the man who does not lose faith in me."*(47)* If we were to lose faith in You it would be disastrous, as we would be losing our contact with the Source of our salvation and our sanctity, including our peace of soul. Thus, we could inversely paraphrase Your statement and say, "Unhappy is the man who loses his faith in Me." Help us to remember also, O Lord, that before we can enter Heaven, we must be purified to the point of perfection either in this life or in Purgatory, since You said in Matthew 5:48 that we must be perfect even as our heavenly Father is perfect.

2. While there could be many things that might lead to the loss of our faith in You, persistent and willful sins are the most common causes. In other words, sins deliberately and repeatedly committed, without contrition and repentance, can lead to a hesitancy to believe in You and finally lead to a total loss of faith. Moreover, when we have lost the gift of faith, we have also lost the gifts of trust (hope) and seed-charity, since they are based on faith. How important it is, then,

to confess our sins immediately afte
committed them.

3. Also the Church encourages us to make frequent sacramental confessions, since we receive not only the assurance of Your forgiveness but an increase of sanctifying grace, which serves to strengthen our faith in You. For these and other reasons the Church encourages us to use the sacrament of Penance for even our venial sins. We strongly believe weekly sacramental confession will give us the grace to overcome all of our sins and faults. *(See "The Catholic Catechism," pp. 495-496, for more on the value of sacramental confession for the forgiveness of venial sins.)*

4. We also noted in today's meditation, Lord, that large numbers of people refused to accept You and the Good News of salvation. Even Your miracles did not move them. *(48)* You implied the root cause of their denial was their intellectual and spiritual pride which darkened their consciences, since they refused to exercise a simple, child-like belief and trust in You. *(49)*

One could reasonably expect that at least those present who were well-educated in religious doctrine, such as the Pharisees and Sadducees, would have easily realized no one could have performed the miracles You did unless You were sent by the Father. Consequently, they should have known Your claims of messiahship were true. But in fact, as You noted, it was mainly the unlearned who received You and Your teachings with that uncomplicated child-like belief and trust You had freely given them. *(50)*

6. Lord, strengthen our faith so we may always accept You as our Messiah. And may we always accept Your teachings as they have been handed down to us in their entirety through Your Catholic Church. *(Read pp. 41-43 of "The Catholic Catechism" on the handing on of divine Revelation through the Catholic Church.)*

7. Most Merciful Redeemer and King, in today's reading You also invite us to approach You with loving faith and trust.

8. "Come to me, all you who labor and are overburdened, and I will give you rest. Shoulder my yoke and learn from me, for I am gentle and humble in heart, and you will find rest for your souls. Yes, my yoke is easy and my burden light." *(51)*

9. Thus, You assure us that when we surrender ourselves to You, placing You first in our lives, then the demands You make of us will in fact not be intolerable because You will be helping us with Your grace.

10. Lord Jesus, we also learned from our meditation how the religious leaders of Your time abused the sabbath day by attaching to it unnecessary and unreasonable laws. So much so, that even healing was prohibited on the grounds it was forbidden by the Old Testament Law. *(52)* But as You pointed out, Lord, this was actually a mistaken interpretation, since God never puts a time limit on performing acts of mercy and other charitable deeds.

11. In our own day, we too can create unnecessary barriers for helping those in need. For instance, we can get so involved in the requirements of our jobs or household duties that we simply neglect to show any real concern for those we know could benefit from our attention. We can even use our jobs as excuses for failing to help others. But if we are honest with ourselves we know this shouldn't be the case. And we should be especially willing to break with routine tasks when it comes to helping those experiencing great anguish. Lord, Your Parable of the Good Samaritan makes this point particularly clear. *(53)*

12.   Most Sacred Heart of Jesus, we also noted in our Scripture reading, the malice of the Pharisees, when in their jealousy and blindness they plotted to put You to death. They even accused You once more of being an agent of the devil, although, in fact, You had cured a blind and dumb possessed person through Your divine power. *(54)*

13.   Finally, Blessed Lord, You spoke of the unforgivable blasphemy against the Holy Spirit. *(55)* Actually, as You well know, the unforgivableness involved here is not God's fault, but the sinner's. There is no sin God will not forgive if we properly repent. Those who, through the hardness of their hearts, repeatedly and habitually reject the promptings of God the Holy Spirit to repent of their sinfulness make forgiveness impossible. May we never allow ourselves to fall into this state! Rather, prompt us to examine our consciences daily with the aid of the Holy Spirit, and inspire us to readily confess our sins with a contrite heart and the desire to amend our lives. And "forgive us our trespasses as we forgive those who trespass against us." Amen.

It is essential you read these Scripture passages and meditations in a reflective manner every day. The Holy Spirit will reveal more insights to you each time you do so. We recommend that you now read Chapter X Paragraphs 79 to 92 of our "Peaceful Seed Living" prayer and meditation book, Volume II.

Words betray the heart

33 "Make a tree sound and its fruit will be (C3)
sound; make a tree rotten and its fruit will be (C2)
rotten. For the tree can be told by its fruit.
34 Brood of vipers, how can your speech be
good when you are evil? For a man's words (C2)
35 flow out of what fills his heart. •A good man
draws good things from his store of good- (C3)
ness; a bad man draws bad things from his (C2)
36 store of badness. •So I tell you this, that for
every unfounded word men utter they will (C2)
37 answer on Judgment day, •since it is by your
words you will be acquitted, and by your (C3)
words condemned." (C2)

38 Then some of the scribes and Pharisees spoke up. "Master," they said "we should
39 like to see a sign[c] from you." ·He replied, "It is an evil and unfaithful generation that asks (C2) for a sign! The only sign it will be given is
40 the sign of the prophet Jonah. ·For as Jonah *was in the belly of the sea-monster for three days and three nights,[d]* so will the Son of Man be in the heart of the earth for three days and
41 three nights. ·On Judgment day the men of Nineveh will stand up with this generation and condemn it, because when Jonah (C2) preached they repented; and there is some- (C2) (C3)
42 thing greater than Jonah here. ·On Judgment day the Queen of the South will rise up with this generation and condemn it, because she (C2) came from the ends of the earth to hear the wisdom of Solomon; and there is something greater than Solomon here.

The return of the unclean spirit

43 "When an unclean spirit goes out of a man (C2) it wanders through waterless country looking
44 for a place to rest, and cannot find one. ·Then it says, 'I will return to the home I came from.' But on arrival, finding it unoccupied,
45 swept and tidied, ·it then goes off and collects seven other spirits more evil than itself, and (C2) they go in and set up house there, so that the man ends up by being worse than he was (C2) before. That is what will happen to this evil (C2) generation."

The true kinsmen of Jesus

46 He was still speaking to the crowds when his mother and his brothers[e] appeared; they were standing outside and were anxious to
48 have a word with him. ·But to the man who told him this Jesus replied, "Who is my
49 mother? Who are my brothers?" ·And stretching out his hand toward his disciples

he said, "Here are my mother and my broth-
50 ers. •Anyone who does the will of my Father
in heaven, he is my brother and sister and
mother."

B. THE SERMON OF PARABLES

Introduction

1 **13** That same day, Jesus left the house and
2 sat by the lakeside, •but such crowds
gathered round him that he got into a boat
and sat there. The people all stood on the
3 beach, •and he told them many things in parables.

Parable of the sower

He said, "Imagine a sower going out to
4 sow. •As he sowed, some seeds fell on the
edge of the path, and the birds came and
5 ate them up. •Others fell on patches of
rock where they found little soil and sprang
up straight away, because there was no
6 depth of earth; •but as soon as the sun came
up they were scorched and, not having
7 any roots, they withered away. •Others
fell among thorns, and the thorns grew

8 up and choked them. •Others fell on rich
soil and produced their crop, some a hun-
9 dredfold, some sixty, some thirty. •Listen,
anyone who has ears!''

Why Jesus speaks in parables

10   Then the disciples went up to him and
asked, "Why do you talk to them in para-
11 bles?'' •"Because,'' he replied, "the mysteries
of the kingdom of heaven are revealed to you,
12 but they are not revealed to them. •For anyone who has will be given more, and he will
have more than enough; but from anyone
who has not, even what he has will be taken
13 away. •The reason I talk to them in parables
is that they look without seeing and listen
14 without hearing or understanding. •So in their
case this prophecy of Isaiah is being fulfilled:

*You will listen and listen again, but not un-
derstand,*
see and see again, but not perceive.
15 *For the heart of this nation has grown coarse,* (C2)
*their ears are dull of hearing, and they have
shut their eyes,*

for fear they should see with their eyes, (C2)
hear with their ears,
understand with their heart, (C1)
and be converted (C2)
and be healed by me.[a] (C3)

16 "But happy are your eyes because they (C3)
17 see, your ears because they hear! ·I tell you
solemnly, many prophets and holy men
longed to see what you see, and never saw (C3)
it; to hear what you hear, and never heard
it.

The parable of the sower explained

18 "You, therefore, are to hear the parable of
the sower.
19 When anyone hears the word of the kingdom without understanding, the evil one
comes and carries off what was sown in his (C2)
heart: this is the man who received the seed
20 on the edge of the path. ·The one who received it on patches of rock is the man who (C1)
hears the word and welcomes it at once with (C3)
21 joy. ·But he has no root in him, he does not (C2)
last; let some trial come, or some persecution
on account of the word, and he falls away at (C2)
22 once. ·The one who received the seed in
thorns is the man who hears the word, but
the worries of this world and the lure of
riches choke the word and so he produces (C2)
23 nothing. ·And the one who received the seed
in rich soil is the man who hears the word (C1)
and understands it; he is the one who yields
a harvest and produces now a hundredfold, (C3)
now sixty, now thirty."

Parable of the darnel

24 He put another parable before them, "The
kingdom of heaven may be compared to a
25 man who sowed good seed in his field. ·While (C3)
everybody was asleep his enemy came,
sowed darnel all among the wheat, and made (C2)

26 off. ·When the new wheat sprouted and rip- (C3)
27 ened, the darnel appeared as well. ·The own- (C2)
er's servants went to him and said, 'Sir, was
it not good seed that you sowed in your field?
If so, where does the darnel come from?'
28 'Some enemy has done this,' he answered. (C2)
And the servants said, 'Do you want us to go
29 and weed it out?' ·But he said, 'No, because
when you weed out the darnel you might pull
30 up the wheat with it. ·Let them both grow till
the harvest; and at harvest time I shall say to
the reapers: First collect the darnel and tie (C2)
it in bundles to be burned, then gather the
wheat into my barn.' " (C3)

Parable of the mustard seed

31   He put another parable before them, "The
kingdom of heaven is like a mustard seed
which a man took and sowed in his field.
32 It is the smallest of all the seeds, but when
it has grown it is the biggest shrub of all and
becomes a tree so that the birds of the air
come and shelter in its branches."

Parable of the yeast

33   He told them another parable, "The kingdom of heaven is like the yeast a woman took
and mixed in with three measures of flour till
it was leavened all through."

105

34 In all this Jesus spoke to the crowds in parables; indeed, he would never speak to 35 them except in parables. •This was to fulfill the prophecy:

I will speak to you in parables
and expound things hidden since the founda-
tion of the world.[b]

The parable of the darnel explained

36 Then, leaving the crowds, he went to the house; and his disciples came to him and said, "Explain the parable about the darnel in the 37 field to us." •He said in reply, "The sower (c3) 38 of the good seed is the Son of Man. •The field is the world; the good seed is the subjects of (c2) the kingdom; the darnel, the subjects of the (c2) 39 evil one; •the enemy who sowed them, the (c2) devil; the harvest is the end of the world; 40 the reapers are the angels. •Well then, just as (c3) the darnel is gathered up and burned in the 41 fire, so it will be at the end of time. •The Son of Man will send his angels and they will gather out of his kingdom all things that pro- 42 voke offenses and all who do evil, •and throw (c2) them into the blazing furnace, where there 43 will be weeping and grinding of teeth. •Then the virtuous will shine like the sun in the (c3) kingdom of their Father.[c] Listen, anyone who has ears!

Parables of the treasure and of the pearl

44 "The kingdom of heaven is like treasure hidden in a field which someone has found; he hides it again, goes off happy, sells every- (c3) thing he owns and buys the field.

45 "Again, the kingdom of heaven is like a 46 merchant looking for fine pearls; •when he (c3) finds one of great value he goes and sells everything he owns and buys it.

47 "Again, the kingdom of heaven is like a dragnet cast into the sea that brings in a haul
48 of all kinds. ·When it is full, the fishermen haul it ashore; then, sitting down, they col- (C2) lect the good ones in a basket and throw (C3)
49 away those that are no use. ·This is how it (C2) will be at the end of time: the angels will (C2) appear and separate the wicked from the just (C3)
50 to throw them into the blazing furnace where there will be weeping and grinding of teeth.

Conclusion

51 "Have you understood all this?" They said,
52 "Yes." ·And he said to them, "Well then, every scribe who becomes a disciple of the (C3) kingdom of heaven is like a householder who brings out from his storeroom things both new and old."[d]

V. THE CHURCH, FIRST-FRUITS OF THE KINGDOM OF HEAVEN

A. NARRATIVE SECTION

A visit to Nazareth

53 When Jesus had finished these parables he
54 left the district; ·and, coming to his home town,[e] he taught the people in their synagogue in such a way that they were astonished and said, "Where did the man get this
55 wisdom and these miraculous powers? ·This is the carpenter's son, surely? Is not his mother the woman called Mary, and his brothers James and Joseph and Simon and
56 Jude? ·His sisters, too, are they not all here with us? So where did the man get it all?"
57 And they would not accept him. But Jesus (C2)

said to them, "A prophet is only despised in
58 his own country and in his own house," •and (C2)
he did not work many miracles there because (C2)
of their lack of faith. (C1)

Week 2 Day 2
Four C's Meditations
on St. Matthew 12:33-13:58

1. Most loving Savior, as we read the
Scripture reading for today, we took special
interest in Your words to the hypocritical,
unrepentant scribes and Pharisees.

2. "Then some of scribes and Pharisees
spoke up. 'Master,' they said 'we should like
to see a sign from you.' He replied, 'It is an
evil and unfaithful generation that asks for a
sign! The only sign it will be given is the sign of
the prophet Jonah. For as Jonah was in the
belly of the sea-monster for three days and
three nights, so will the Son of Man be in the
heart of the earth for three days and three
nights. On Judgment day the men of Nineveh

will stand up with this generation and condemn it, because when Jonah preached they repented; and there is something greater than Jonah here. On Judgment day the Queen of the South will rise up with this generation and condemn it, because she came from the ends of the earth to hear the wisdom of Solomon; and there is something greater than Solomon here.' " *(56)*

3. Jesus, You also faulted the scribes and Pharisees on other occasions for their refusal to see themselves as sinners in need of divine help. *(57)* Sadly then, when they were in this frame of mind they could not receive divine forgiveness and friendship.

4. This truth, Most Merciful Lord, led us to reflect on the fact that many parents also lead lives which fail to show signs of genuine repentance and seed-charity. Moreover, children are usually quick to notice this and often imitate their parents in this regard. At

other times, children, especially when being disciplined, or threatened with discipline, point out in concrete terms to their parents that they too are less than perfect. And regretfully, many parents then often offer some lame excuse for their improper conduct. Consequently, just like the scribes and Pharisees, such parents, being satisfied with their own behavior, find themselves increasingly open to the influence of the demonic spirits which You alluded to in our meditation.

5. "When an unclean spirit goes out of a man it wanders through waterless country looking for a place to rest, and cannot find one. Then it says, 'I will return to the home I came from.' But on arrival, finding it unoccupied, swept and tidied, it then goes off and collects seven other spirits more evil then itself, and they go in and set up house there, so that the man ends up by being worse than he was before. This is what will happen to this evil generation."*(58)*

6. How important it is then, Lord, for parents, as well as for all of us, to examine our consciences daily, and confess our sins, and to receive the sacrament of Penance on a regular basis; hopefully once a week. Children who observe that their parents, though not perfect, are striving with Your grace to become perfect, are apt to be more inclined to strive for Christian perfection themselves.

7. Holy Mary and Joseph, help parents to

acknowledge their need for a constant dependence upon Jesus to fulfill their parental vocation. How much, as His disciples and representatives, they need to pray, repent, amend their lives and make use of the abundant graces found in the sacraments, especially in Matrimony, the Eucharist and Penance. In times of family trials, spouses should call on God to give them increases in the graces of the sacrament of Matrimony. May they resemble the good trees Jesus spoke of which bear sound fruit. (59) And may they always see Your divine Son as the Source of their happiness and joy. Moreover, may they always willingly receive His doctrine, especially as it is explained and taught by the Successor of Peter, the Pope, and those bishops who teach in communion with him as their head.

8.   Most Sacred Heart of Jesus, help all family members to confide in You and to sow seeds of self-sacrifice as cooperators and imitators of the Holy Family.

9.   Lord, the Parables You taught were like spiritual seeds sown into the souls of those who believed in You with loving hearts.

10.   "The reason I talk to them in parables is that they look without seeing and listen without hearing or understanding. So in their case this prophecy of Isaiah is being fulfilled: 'You will listen and listen again, but not understand, see and see again, but not perceive. For the heart of this nation has grown coarse, their ears are dull of hearing,

111

and they have shut their eyes, for fear they should see with their eyes, hear with their ears, understand with their heart, and be converted and be healed by me.' But happy are your eyes because they see, your ears because they hear! I tell you solemnly, many prophets and holy men longed to see what you see, and never say it; to hear what you hear, and never heard it."*(60)*

11.   Those with pure hearts received these parable-seeds and allowed them to germinate in their souls. Sometimes they continued to grow through prayer and meditation, causing their meaning to become increasingly apparent. At other times, You made things less difficult for the pure in heart by clearly revealing the message You wished to convey, as You did in the case of the Parable of the Sower.*(61)* On the other hand, those who did not accept You and the Gospel, received no more than a mysterious parable. For them it

had no real meaning and their hearts remained hardened. Consequently, they continued to court eternal damnation.

12.   Lord, help us to be always receptive to Your teaching as it comes to us through Your Holy Catholic Church. It is only through this doctrine that the real meaning of our lives can be found. And it is only in the reception and living out of Your teaching that true happiness is to be found in this life and in the next.

13.   In reference to the Parable of the Sower, Jesus, You pointed out there are some who never receive the saving doctrine of the Kingdom of Heaven because of their sinful hearts. Whether they realize it or not, they become subjects of satan's kingdom. Others receive Your teaching and it takes root and grows with the passage of time. But among these persons it is only those who persevere in the Christian life of faith, trust and seed-charity who bear the spiritual fruit of sanctity, interior peace and joy; some more, some less, according to their efforts and God's grace.

14.   Lord, assist us always in performing deeds of charity, compassion and sacrifice. And remind us to do this especially within our own families, since as families increasingly reflect the unselfish charity of the Holy Family, the world becomes more holy and the Church itself prospers according to Your will.

15.   Every seed of charity sown for the sake of the advancement of Your heavenly

Kingdom is like the mustard seed or the yeast mentioned in Your parables. *(62)* They will grow and multiply and stimulate further acts of charity, each one becoming a building stone of Your Kingdom, which is partly present even now on earth. *(For more information on the nature of this kingdom, read pp. 208-209, in "The Catholic Catechism.")*

16. Jesus, You also clearly taught us in today's reading that You are not the only one who sows seeds. The devil does as well. Many of his seeds take root, sprout and bear deformed and unpalatable fruit for his eternal kingdom of darkness and suffering. As St. Peter has taught us, no one should consider himself immune from demonic temptations in this life. *(63)* We must always be on guard against them, and if they have led us to commit sins, we must expel them with a sincere confession.

17.   Most Sacred Heart of Jesus, we always need to be open to the good seeds of Your doctrine and grace thereby preparing ourselves for a destiny of unending happiness in Your presence. Therefore, help us to regard Your Kingdom as a pearl of great value for which we would sacrifice everything, if necessary, to obtain it. (64)

18.   Finally, Merciful Lord, in our meditation our attention dwelt on those who would not accept You as being any more than a man, in spite of Your extraordinary wisdom and miraculous powers.

19.   "When Jesus had finished these parables he left the district; and, coming to his home town, he taught the people in their synagogue in such a way that they were astonished and said, 'Where did the man get this wisdom and these miraculous powers? This is the carpenter's son, surely? Is not his mother the woman called Mary, and his brothers James and Joseph and Simon and Jude? His sisters, too, are they not all here with us? So where did the man get it all?' And they would not accept him. But Jesus said to them, 'A prophet is only despised in his own country and in his own house,' and he did not work many miracles there *because of their lack of faith.*" (65)

20.   Today, Lord, there are also many who tend to see You only as a man, refusing to acknowledge Your divinity. For this reason, they cannot adore You at Mass or elsewhere, since adoration is reserved only for God.

21.   Please assist us in helping such people acknowledge You as the eternal Son of God, made man, so they can consciously and joyfully receive You as the Source of their salvation and derive those benefits reserved for those who worship You in spirit and in truth.

22.   Jesus Christ, Son of God, have mercy on us sinners. Amen.

Try to re-read and meditate on these Scripture passages and reflections at least one more time today.

At this time, please slowly read Chapter XI, Paragraphs 1 to 20 of our "Peaceful Seed Living" prayer and meditation book, Volume II.

Herod and Jesus

1 **14** At that time Herod the tetrarch heard
2 about the reputation of Jesus, ·and said
to his court, "This is John the Baptist himself;
he has risen from the dead, and that is why
miraculous powers are at work in him."

John the Baptist beheaded

3 Now it was Herod who had arrested John, (C 2)
chained him up and put him in prison because
4 of Herodias, his brother Philip's*a* wife. ·For (C3)
John had told him, "It is against the Law for
5 you to have her." ·He had wanted to kill him (C3)
but was afraid of the people, who regarded (C2)
6 John as a prophet. ·Then, during the celebra-
tions for Herod's birthday, the daughter of
Herodias*b* danced before the company, and
7 so delighted Herod ·that he promised on oath
8 to give her anything she asked. ·Prompted by
her mother she said, "Give me John the Bap- (C2)
9 tist's head, here, on a dish." ·The king was
distressed but, thinking of the oaths he had (C 2)
sworn and of his guests, he ordered it to be
10 given her, ·and sent and had John beheaded (C 2)
11 in the prison. ·The head was brought in on
a dish and given to the girl who took it to her (C2)
12 mother. ·John's disciples came and took the
body and buried it; then they went off to tell (C3)
Jesus.

First miracle of the loaves

13 When Jesus received this news he withdrew by boat to a lonely place where they
could be by themselves. But the people heard
of this and, leaving the towns, went after him
14 on foot. ·So as he stepped ashore he saw a

large crowd; and he took pity on them and (C3)
healed their sick.

15 When evening came, the disciples went to him and said, "This is a lonely place, and the time has slipped by; so send the people away, and they can go to the villages to buy them-
16 selves some food." •Jesus replied, "There is no need for them to go: give them something (C3)
17 to eat yourselves." •But they answered, "All we have with us is five loaves and two fish."
19 "Bring them here to me," he said. •He gave orders that the people were to sit down on the grass; then he took the five loaves and the two fish, raised his eyes to heaven and said the blessing. And breaking the loaves he handed them to his disciples who gave them
20 to the crowds. •They all ate as much as they wanted, and they collected the scraps remain-
21 ing, twelve baskets full. •Those who ate numbered about five thousand men, to say nothing of women and children.

Jesus walks on the water and, with him, Peter

22 Directly after this he made the disciples get into the boat and go on ahead to the other side while he would send the crowds away.
23 After sending the crowds away he went up into the hills by himself to pray. When eve- (C3)

24 ning came, he was there alone, •while the boat, by now far out on the lake, was battling with a heavy sea, for there was a headwind. 25 In the fourth watch of the night[c] he went 26 toward them, walking on the lake, •and when the disciples saw him walking on the lake they were terrified. "It is a ghost," they said, 27 and cried out in fear. •But at once Jesus called out to them, saying, "Courage! It is I! Do not 28 be afraid." •It was Peter who answered. "Lord," he said, "if it is you, tell me to come (C1) 29 to you across the water." •"Come," said Jesus. Then Peter got out of the boat and started walking toward Jesus across the wa- (C3) 30 ter, •but as soon as he felt the force of the wind, he took fright and began to sink. "Lord! (C1) 31 Save me!" he cried. •Jesus put out his hand at once and held him. "Man of little faith," (C1) 32 he said, "why did you doubt?" •And as they (C2) 33 got into the boat the wind dropped. •The men in the boat bowed down before him and said, "Truly, you are the Son of God." (C1)

Cures at Gennesaret

34 Having made the crossing, they came to 35 land at Gennesaret. •When the local people recognized him they spread the news through the whole neighborhood and took all that (C1) 36 were sick to him, •begging him just to let them touch the fringe of his cloak. And (C3) all those who touched it were completely (C3) cured.

The traditions of the Pharisees

1 **15** Pharisees and scribes from Jerusalem 2 then came to Jesus and said, •"Why do your disciples break away from the tradition of the elders?[a] They do not wash their hands 3 when they eat food." •"And why do you," he answered, "break away from the command- (C2) ment of God for the sake of your tradition? 4 For God said: *Do your duty to[b] your father* (C3) *and mother* and: *Anyone who curses father or* (C2)

119

5 *mother must be put to death.*[c] •But you say,
'If anyone says to his father or mother: Anything I have that I might have used to help
6 you is dedicated to God,' •he is rid of his duty (C2)
to father or mother.[d] In this way you have
made God's word null and void by means of
7 your tradition. •Hypocrites! It was you Isaiah (C2)
meant when he so rightly prophesied:

8 *This people honors me only with lip-service,* (C2)
while their hearts are far from me.

9 *The worship they offer me is worthless;* (C2)
the doctrines they teach are only human regulations."[e]

On clean and unclean

10 He called the people to him and said, "Lis-
11 ten, and understand. •What goes into the
mouth does not make a man unclean; it is
what comes out of the mouth that makes him (C2)
unclean."

12 Then the disciples came to him and said,
"Do you know that the Pharisees were
shocked when they heard what you said?" (C2)
13 He replied, "Any plant my heavenly Father
has not planted will be pulled up by the roots. (C2)
14 Leave them alone. They are blind men lead- (C2)

ing blind men; and if one blind man leads another, both will fall into a pit."

15 At this, Peter said to him, "Explain the
16 parable for us." •Jesus replied, "Do even you
17 not yet understand? •Can you not see that whatever goes into the mouth passes through the stomach and is discharged into the sewer?
18 But the things that come out of the mouth come from the heart, and it is these that make
19 a man unclean. •For from the heart come evil (C2) intentions: murder, adultery, fornication, (C2)
20 theft, perjury, slander. •These are the things that make a man unclean. But to eat with unwashed hands does not make a man unclean."

The daughter of the Canaanite woman healed

21 Jesus left that place and withdrew to the
22 region of Tyre and Sidon. •Then out came a Canaanite woman from that district and started shouting, "Sir, Son of David, take pity (C1) on me. My daughter is tormented by a devil." (C2)
23 But he answered her not a word. And his disciples went and pleaded with him. "Give her what she wants," they said, "because she
24 is shouting after us." •He said in reply, "I was sent only to the lost sheep of the House of
25 Israel." •But the woman had come up and was kneeling at his feet. "Lord," she said,
26 "help me." •He replied, "It is not fair to take (C1) the children's food and throw it to the house-
27 dogs." •She retorted, "Ah yes, sir; but even house-dogs can eat the scraps that fall from
28 their master's table." •Then Jesus answered her, "Woman, you have great faith. Let your (C1) wish be granted." And from that moment her (C3) daughter was well again.

Cures near the lake

29 Jesus went on from there and reached the shores of the Sea of Galilee, and he went up
30 into the hills. He sat there, •and large crowds

121

came to him bringing the lame, the crippled, (C3)
the blind, the dumb and many others; these
they put down at his feet, and he cured them. (C3)
31 The crowds were astonished to see the dumb
speaking, the cripples whole again, the lame
walking and the blind with their sight, and
they praised the God of Israel. (C3)

Second miracle of the loaves

32 But Jesus called his disciples to him and
said, "I feel sorry for all these people; they (C3)
have been with me for three days now and
have nothing to eat. I do not want to send
them off hungry, they might collapse on the (C3)
33 way." ·The disciples said to him, "Where
could we get enough bread in this deserted
34 place to feed such a crowd?" ·Jesus said to
them, "How many loaves have you?"
"Seven," they said, "and a few small fish."
35 Then he instructed the crowd to sit down on
36 the ground, ·and he took the seven loaves and
the fish, and he gave thanks and broke them (C3)
and handed them to the disciples who gave
37 them to the crowds. ·They all ate as much as
they wanted, and they collected what was left
38 of the scraps, seven baskets full. ·Now four
thousand men had eaten, to say nothing of

³⁹ women and children. ·And when he had sent the crowds away he got into the boat and went to the district of Magadan.

Week 2 Day 3
Four C's Meditations
on St. Matthew 14:1-15:39

1. In this meditation, Lord, we learned of St. John the Baptist's extraordinary faith in God, and also of his heroic seed-charity, evidenced by his martyrdom.*(66)* Unlike many of the Pharisees, St. John was determined to defend the divine commandments, even if he had to forfeit his life in the process. Accusing Herod of adultery for marrying the wife of his living half brother, John was chained, imprisoned and finally beheaded. Here we find his faith and his love of God put to the supreme test. *(See "The Catholic Catechism," pp. 181-182, for a discussion on Christian suffering and martyrdom.)*

2. John could have simply excused Herod

since, in fact, he had not broken the Roman civil law. Thus, John could have saved his own life. But what would have been his fate at the hands of God when he would ultimately be brought to account for his failure to castigate Herod for breaking God's law?

3. Jesus, we also must witness to the sanctity of marriage. You have ordained that all divinely-sanctioned marriages are indissoluble. That is, by nature they may not be broken except by death. In the case of Christian marriage, which is a sacrament, You have additionally taught that, unlike the Old Testament period, there are to be no exceptions to the rule of indissolublity. Therefore, help those who are married, Lord, to remain faithful to their spouses until death. And help Christians make the proper use of the grace they receive through this sacrament, so they will be able to love one another sacrificially until death. *(For discussion of Jesus' teaching on the indissolubility of marriage, read pp. 365-367 of "The Catholic Catechism.")*

4. In a society that is increasingly pagan, help us Jesus, to bear constant witness to the indissolubility of marriage, thus setting the right example for our children, for our neighbors, for our parish, and for society at large.

5. Next in our reading, Blessed Lord, Matthew describes that memorable account of Peter's wavering faith in You. As You walked across the lake towards him, You assured Peter and the others, that it was indeed You

and not a ghost. Still uncertain, however, Peter cried out, "Lord, if it is you, tell me to come to you across the water."(67) You then commanded him to come to You, and exercising belief and trust in You , he began his miraculous walk. But shortly thereafter, his confidence weakened and he began to sink, crying out to You for help. You responded by reaching out and holding him, pronouncing him to be a man of little faith.(68)

6. Surely, Jesus, many of us are more like the wavering Peter than like the steadfast and courageous John the Baptist. John's confidence in You was full and enduring. Peter's was often very weak, and at times this man, who was destined to become the head of the Church, came close to rejecting You completely.(69)

7. As with Peter, it is usually when we suffer

as Christians that our trust and loyalty in You tend to waver. But such suffering is providentially allowed so we might grow in sanctity. It is especially true that when we persevere in confidence and seed-charity during times of trial, we increase in saintly virtue and bear much spiritual fruit, benefiting not only ourselves, but also others, including those who cause us to suffer.

8. Thankfully, Jesus, You promised You will never forsake us, no matter what the circumstances, as long as we turn to You in confidence and in charity. "And know that I am with you always; yes, to the end of time."(70) Lord, inscribe these words deeply in our hearts.

9. We know temptations must come. But thankfully You have promised us with every temptation You will provide a way to resist.(71) You have also assured us that if we are steadfast in our faith, trust and sacrificial love until the end, we will be saved.(72)

10. Also in today's reading, Lord, You pointed out how the scribes and Pharisees deviated from the divine commandments.(73) And in our own times, we detect the same tendency in certain quarters. For instance, there are those within the Church who dissent from Your commandments as presented to us by Scripture and Sacred Tradition and ennunciated particularly by the Pope, who is Your chief spiritual representative on earth. And if we observe carefully, that which

modern dissenters usually affirm in place of Your doctrine, is that which requires less sacrifice and is more in keeping with popular non-Catholic opinion. *(For a detailed presentation on the nature and role of Scripture and Tradition in the Church, read pp., 41-42 in "The Catholic Catechism.")*

11. However, following You, Lord, at all times was not meant to be especially easy. Nonetheless, it was meant to be rewarding in terms of sanctity and interior peace and happiness. Yours was the Way of the Cross; ours also must be the Way of the Cross; conquering our sinful tendencies, persevering in our trials, and faithfully fulfilling our God-given responsibilities by sacrificing our will to Yours. And once we die as a seed to our self-ishness You will give us that inner peace the world cannot give.

12.   Most Sacred Heart of Jesus, in today's meditation, we noted with interest the great faith the non-Jewish woman from Canaan had in You when she asked You to heal her demoniac daughter. *(74)* Her example showed the Jewish onlookers that even people without the benefit of Old Testament membership could believe You were the Messiah, whom the prophets had predicted centuries earlier.

13.   Lord, in our own day, many of us Catholics can immediately think of non-Catholic friends and acquaintances who have such extraordinary faith and trust in You, that we are often put to shame. May their examples encourage us to seek even greater faith and trust in You. And, in return, may we take advantage of every oportunity to share the fullness of the Catholic Faith with them.

14.   Jesus, Mary and Joseph, help us, the Apostolate, and all the members of our families to realize that only through a God-centered life can we find peace and true security. Amen.

Try to experience God's gift of peace, through the action of the Holy Spirit, by slowly re-reading and meditating on the Scripture for today.

Now refer to Chapter XI, Paragraphs 21 to 22; and Chapter XII, Introduction Paragraphs 1 to 14; of our "Peaceful Seed Living" prayer and meditation book, Volume II.

WEEK 2 DAY 4
The Gospel of St. Matthew
Chapter 16:1-17:27

The Pharisees ask for a sign from heaven

1 **16** The Pharisees and Sadducees came, and to test him they asked if he would ((C2)
2 show them a sign from heaven. •He replied, "In the evening you say, 'It will be fine; there
3 is a red sky,' •and in the morning, 'Stormy weather today; the sky is red and overcast.' You know how to read the face of the sky, but you cannot read the signs of the times. ((C2)
4 It is an evil and unfaithful generation that ((C2) asks for a sign! The only sign it will be given is the sign of Jonah." And leaving them ((C2) standing here, he went away.

The yeast of the Pharisees and Sadducees

5 The disciples, having crossed to the other
6 shore, had forgotten to take any food. •Jesus said to them, "Keep your eyes open, and be on your guard against the yeast of the Phari- ((C2)
7 sees and Sadducees." •And they said to themselves, "It is because we have not
8 brought any bread." •Jesus knew it, and he said, "Men of little faith, why are you talking ((C1) ((C2) among yourselves about having no bread?
9 Do you not yet understand? Do you not remember the five loaves for the five thousand and the number of baskets you col-
10 lected? •Or the seven loaves for the four thousand and the number of baskets you col-
11 lected? •How could you fail to understand that I was not talking about bread? What I said was: Beware of the yeast of the Pharisees ((C2)
12 and Sadducees." •Then they understood that he was telling them to be on their guard, not

129

against the yeast for making bread, but against the teaching of the Pharisees and Sadducees.*a* (C2)

Peter's profession of faith; his pre-eminence

13   When Jesus came to the region of Caesarea Philippi he put this question to his disciples, "Who do people say the Son of Man
14 is?" •And they said, "Some say he is John the Baptist, some Elijah, and others Jeremiah or
15 one of the prophets." •"But you," he said,
16 "who do you say I am?" •Then Simon Peter spoke up, "You are the Christ," he said, "the
17 Son of the living God." •Jesus replied, "Simon son of Jonah, you are a happy man! Because it was not flesh and blood that revealed this to you but my Father in heaven.
18 So I now say to you: You are Peter*b* and on this rock I will build my Church. And the gates of the underworld*c* can never hold out
19 against it. •I will give you the keys of the kingdom of heaven: whatever you bind on earth shall be considered bound in heaven; whatever you loose on earth shall be consid-
20 ered loosed in heaven."*d* •Then he gave the disciples strict orders not to tell anyone that he was the Christ.

130

21 From that time Jesus began to make it clear to his disciples that he was destined to go to Jerusalem and suffer grievously at the (C2) hands of the elders and chief priests and scribes, to be put to death and to be raised (C2)
22 up on the third day. ·Then, taking him aside, Peter started to remonstrate with him. "Heaven preserve you, Lord"; he said, "this (C2)
23 must not happen to you." ·But he turned and said to Peter, "Get behind me, Satan! You are an obstacle in my path, because the way (C2) you think is not God's way but man's."

The condition of following Christ

24 Then Jesus said to his disciples, "If anyone wants to be a follower of mine, let him re- (C3) nounce himself and take up his cross and
25 follow me. ·For anyone who wants to save his life will lose it; but anyone who loses his (C2)
26 life for my sake will find it. ·What, then, will (C3) a man gain if he wins the whole world and ruins his life? Or what has a man to offer in (C2) exchange for his life?
27 "For the Son of Man is going to come in the glory of his Father with his angels, and, when he does, he will reward each one
28 according to his behavior. ·I tell you solemnly, there are some of these standing here who will not taste death before they see the Son of Man coming with his kingdom.'ᵉ

The transfiguration

1 **17** Six days later, Jesus took with him Peter and James and his brother John and led them up a high mountain where they
2 could be alone. ·There in their presence he was transfigured: his face shone like the sun and his clothes became as white as the light.
3 Suddenly Moses and Elijahᵃ appeared to
4 them; they were talking with him. ·Then

Peter spoke to Jesus. "Lord," he said, "it is wonderful for us to be here; if you wish, I will make three tents here, one for you, one for (C3) 5 Moses and one for Elijah." ·He was still speaking when suddenly a bright cloud covered them with shadow, and from the cloud there came a voice which said, "This is my Son, the Beloved; he enjoys my favor. Listen 6 to him." ·When they heard this, the disciples 7 fell on their faces, overcome with fear. ·But Jesus came up and touched them. "Stand 8 up," he said, "do not be afraid." ·And when they raised their eyes they saw no one but only Jesus.

The question about Elijah

9 As they came down from the mountain Jesus gave them this order, "Tell no one about the vision until the Son of Man has 10 risen from the dead." ·And the disciples put this question to him, "Why do the scribes say 11 then that Elijah has to come first?" ·"True"; he replied, "Elijah is to come to see that everything is once more as it should be; 12 however, I tell you that Elijah has come already and they did not recognize him but treated him as they pleased; and the Son of

13 Man will suffer similarly at their hands." •The (C2)
disciples understood then that he had been
speaking of John the Baptist.

The epileptic demoniac

14   As they were rejoining the crowd a man
came up to him and went down on his knees
15 before him. •"Lord," he said "take pity on my (C1)
son: he is a lunatic and in a wretched state; (C3)
he is always falling into the fire or into the
16 water. •I took him to your disciples and they
17 were unable to cure him." •"Faithless and
perverse generation!" Jesus said in reply, (C2)
"How much longer must I be with you? How
much longer must I put up with you? Bring
18 him here to me." •And when Jesus rebuked (C3)
it the devil came out of the boy who was (C2)
cured from that moment.
19   Then the disciples came privately to Jesus.
"Why were we unable to cast it out?" they
20 asked. •He answered, "Because you have lit- (C1)
tle faith. I tell you solemnly, if your faith were (C1)
the size of a mustard seed you could say to
this mountain, 'Move from here to there,' and
it would move; nothing would be impossible
for you."

Second prophecy of the Passion

22   One day when they were together in Galilee, Jesus said to them, "The Son of Man is
going to be handed over into the power of (C2)
23 men; •they will put him to death, and on the (C2)
third day he will be raised to life again." And
a great sadness came over them. (C3)

The Temple tax paid by Jesus and Peter

24   When they reached Capernaum, the collectors of the half-shekel*b* came to Peter and
said, "Does your master not pay the half-
25 shekel?" •"Oh yes," he replied, and went into
the house. But before he could speak, Jesus

said, "Simon, what is your opinion? From whom do the kings of the earth take toll or tribute? From their sons or from foreigners?"

26 And when he replied, "From foreigners," Jesus said, "Well then, the sons are exempt.

27 However, so as not to offend these people, (C3) go to the lake and cast a hook; take the first fish that bites, open its mouth and there you will find a shekel; take it and give it to them for me and for you."

Week 2 Day 4
Four C's Meditations
on St. Matthew 16:1-17:27

1. Most holy and compassionate Jesus, during Your public ministry on earth, You were constantly pursued by Your enemies. Among them, of course, were the Pharisees and Sadducees. In today's meditation, members of both of these religious parties confronted You by asking for a sign of Your divinity and messiahship. You rightly refused to oblige them since they already had ample opportunity to confirm this for themselves

from their prior observation of Your many healing miracles and exorcisms. Their spiritual blindness, however, had prevented them from doing so.

2. Jesus, keep our spiritual vision free from the darkness of sin, so we may always acknowledge Your divinity and messiahship. And remind us, from time to time, that You are actually present in the hearts of those who are free from the stain of mortal sin. But You are present in a particularly effective way in the Holy Eucharist. Moreover, You promised us You would also be present whenever two or three people are gathered together in Your Name. You have taught us, too, that You are present in the poor, in strangers, in the hungry and the afflicted.(75) And when we help them, we are helping You.(76)

3. Lord, may we always help the needy, especially those of our own families. Help us to sow true seeds of charity in their lives.

135

Also, we praise and thank You, Jesus, for the innumerable times we have received Your selfless love which continually flows from Your Most Sacred Heart.

4. Lord Jesus, help us to avoid the yeast of false teaching. That is, the heresy for which You condemned the Pharisees and Sadducees in today's Scripture reading.(77) Heresy, which always misrepresents You or Your Gospel, acts like yeast since it starts out usually in one place and with one person or with a group of persons. And it is not long before it branches out, infesting multitudes with its poison. Thankfully, You gave Your followers a sure safeguard against heresy when You provided Your Church with the infallible teaching office of the Pope and the bishops in union with him as their head. *(For a detailed discussion on this teaching office read pp. 224-233 of "The Catholic Catechism.")*

5. Lord, it was with the gift of faith, given him by Your Father, that St. Peter was able to confess You as the divine Messiah.(78) And we are grateful that You bestow this gift on all who ask for it and strengthen it in those who believe with a sincere heart. Since we live in the midst of so much doubt and outright denial of Your divinity and messiahship, we beg You to maintain and increase our faith in You daily.

6. It is one thing, Lord, to believe You are the divine Messiah as Peter did, but it is quite another to always understand Your will for us

136

as unique individuals. For instance, we often do not understand why we must face some particular suffering and evil which are not of our own making. Yet we must continually have confidence (faith and trust) in You as the One Who provides for us and guides our lives, even when we are in very trying circumstances.

7.   We must always keep in mind that after the sorrow of Your suffering and Crucifixion, You experienced the joy of the Resurrection and accomplished our salvation. And we must believe as You have promised, that You and the Father will not abandon us in our troubles, if we persevere in our love for You.*(79)* As a matter of fact, You will enable us to emerge as stronger and better Christians. Not only that, even when we are experiencing our sorrows and tragedies, if we persevere in Your love, we will also experience Your inner peace.*(80)*

8.   Nor should we forget that some of the suffering we face in this life may be of our own making due to our sins. But whatever the cause, You command us to take up our crosses daily and follow You. *(81)* We must be willing to undergo suffering and hardships, if the circumstances require it. This attitude involves a willingness to die to self-will and a deep desire to live for You and Your will. And it is this attitude that fosters peaceful seed-living.

9.   Jesus, the more we foresake our will for Yours, the more we find lasting satisfaction and happiness in this life. The truth of this is obvious when we think of those who live primarily for themselves. They are unhappy, miserable and lonely. On the other hand, the saints are happy because, with Your help, they have learned to conquer their self-will.

10.   Lord, in today's Scripture reading, You rebuked Your disciples for their failure to expel the demons possessing an unfortunate demoniac. *(82)* The root of their difficulty was not possessing enough faith. Increase our faith in You so we can accomplish great things for the glory of God the Father and for Your Kingdom.

11.   If we stop to think of the saints and those who lead saintly lives today, we see they have accomplished great things because of their tremendous faith and trust in You. Moreover, many of these God-centered people had great handicaps and obstacles to overcome, such as the opposition of friends

and foes, sickness, frail bodies, and often, their own fears. Lord, You will never fail to give large amounts of faith and trust to those who seek it in humility and charity. You are the Source of our spiritual strength.

12. "I tell you solemnly, if your faith (confidence) were the size of a mustard seed, you could say to this mountain, 'Move from here to there,' and it would move: nothing would be impossible for you." *(83)*

13. Lord Jesus, always increase our faith and hope in You. And that we may constantly love You in Whom we believe and trust, never deprive us of the great gift of seed-charity. Amen.

Read these Scripture passages and meditations in a reflective manner every day. The Holy Spirit will reveal more insights to you each time you do so.

You can now refer to Chapter XII, Paragraphs 15 to 34 of our "Peaceful Seed Living" prayer and meditation book, Volume II.

B. THE DISCOURSE
ON THE CHURCH

Who is the greatest?

1 **18** At this time the disciples came to Jesus and said, "Who is the greatest in the
2 kingdom of heaven?" •So he called a little (C3)
child to him and set the child in front of them.
3 Then he said, "I tell you solemnly, unless (C1)
you change and become like little children (C2)
you will never enter the kingdom of heaven. (C3)
4 And so, the one who makes himself as little
as this little child is the greatest in the king- (C3)
dom of heaven.

On leading others astray

5 "Anyone who welcomes a little child like
6 this in my name welcomes me. •But anyone (C3)
who is an obstacle to bring down one of these (C2)
little ones who have faith in me would be ·(C1)
better drowned in the depths of the sea with
7 a great millstone round his neck. •Alas for the
world that there should be such obstacles! (C2)
Obstacles indeed there must be, but alas for (C2)
the man who provides them! (C2)
8 "If your hand or your foot should cause (C2)
you to sin, cut it off and throw it away: it is
better for you to enter into life crippled or
lame, than to have two hands or two feet and
9 be thrown into eternal fire. •And if your eye
should cause you to sin, tear it out and throw
it away: it is better for you to enter into life (C2)
with one eye, than to have two eyes and be
thrown into the hell of fire.
10 "See that you never despise any of these (C2)
little ones, for I tell you that their angels in

140

heaven are continually in the presence of my Father in heaven.[a]

The lost sheep

12 "Tell me. Suppose a man has a hundred sheep and one of them strays; will he not leave the ninety-nine on the hillside and go 13 in search of the stray? •I tell you solemnly, if he finds it, it gives him more joy than do 14 the ninety-nine that did not stray at all. •Similarly, it is never the will of your Father in heaven that one of these little ones should be (C3) lost. (C2)

Brotherly correction

15 "If your brother does something wrong, (C2) go and have it out with him alone, between (C3) your two selves. If he listens to you, you have 16 won back your brother. •If he does not listen, (C3) take one or two others along with you: *the evidence of two or three witnesses is required* 17 *to sustain any charge.* •But if he refuses to (C2) listen to these, report it to the community;[b] (C3) and if he refuses to listen to the community, treat him like a pagan or a tax collector. (C3)

141

18 "I tell you solemnly, whatever you bind on
earth shall be considered bound in heaven;
whatever you loose on earth shall be considered loosed in heaven.

Prayer in common

19 "I tell you solemnly once again, if two of
you on earth agree to ask anything at all, it
will be granted to you by my Father in
20 heaven. •For where two or three meet in my
name, I shall be there with them."

Forgiveness of injuries

21 Then Peter went up to him and said.
"Lord, how often must I forgive my brother (C3)
if he wrongs me? As often as seven times?" (C4)
22 Jesus answered, "Not seven, I tell you, but
seventy-seven times.

Parable of the unforgiving debtor

23 "And so the kingdom of heaven may be
compared to a king who decided to settle his
24 accounts with his servants. •When the reckoning began, they brought him a man who
25 owed ten thousand talents;*c* •but he had no
means of paying, so his master gave orders
that he should be sold, together with his wife
and children and all his possessions, to meet
26 the debt. •At this, the servant threw himself
down at his master's feet. 'Give me time,' he
27 said, 'and I will pay the whole sum.' •And the
servant's master felt so sorry for him that he (C3)
28 let him go and cancelled the debt. •Now as
this servant went out, he happened to meet
a fellow servant who owed him one hundred
denarii;*d* and he seized him by the throat and
began to throttle him. 'Pay what you owe me,' (C2)
29 he said. •His fellow servant fell at his feet and
implored him, saying, 'Give me time and I
30 will pay you.' •But the other would not agree; (C2)
on the contrary, he had him thrown into (C2)

142

31 prison till he should pay the debt. •His fellow servants were deeply distressed when they (C3) saw what had happened, and they went to their master and reported the whole affair to
32 him. •Then the master sent for him. 'You (C2) wicked servant,' he said. 'I cancelled all that debt of yours when you appealed to me. (C3)
33 Were you not bound, then, to have pity on your fellow servant just as I had pity on you?' (C3)
34 And in his anger the master handed him over to the torturers till he should pay all his debt.
35 And that is how my heavenly Father will deal with you unless you each forgive your (C3) brother from your heart.''

Week 2 Day 5
Four C's Meditations
on St. Matthew 18:1-35

1. "Who is the greatest in the kingdom of heaven?"(84) This question put to You by Your disciples, Lord, was answered with the aid of a small child. Placing the child in front of You, You said, "I tell you solemnly, unless you change and become like little children, you will never enter the kingdom of heaven. And so, the one who makes himself as little as this little child is the greatest in the kingdom of heaven."(85)

2. The basic child-like quality You had in mind was that of a simple and complete belief and trust in You as the Source of our mental, material and spiritual well-being. This is a belief and trust which knows no doubts or waverings. Such a person knows You love him and that You will do everything necessary to secure his well-being in this life and in the next. He also knows You love others too and that You will provide for their welfare as well, insofar as they offer You no resistance.

3. Jesus, we humbly ask You to remove our doubts and our wavering trust in You. Give us that simple belief and trust children are known to possess.

4. Yet with respect to children, especially small children, it is precisely because they are so believing and trusting that they can be easily led astray by those who appear to be

credible and trustworthy, but in fact are not. Here, Lord, the importance of example becomes obvious. Older brothers and sisters, especially, are imitated by those younger than themselves. It is crucial, therefore, that not only adults but also older children set the proper Christian example for younger children. Many, perhaps most, young children are more easily led by example, good or bad, than by long and reasoned arguments in favor of the Faith.

5.   Most Sacred Heart of Jesus, in today's Scripture reading, You also make it abundantly clear, and in startlingly dramatic terms, that whatever might cause young children to lose their faith in You should be removed immediately.

6.   "Anyone who welcomes a little child like this in my name welcomes me. But anyone who is an obstacle to bring down one of these little ones who have faith in me would be better drowned in the depths of the sea with a great millstone round his neck. Alas, for the world that there should be such obstacles! Obstacles indeed there must be, but alas for the man who provides them! If your hand or your foot should cause you to sin, cut it off and throw it away: it is better for you to enter into life crippled or lame, than to have two hands or two feet and be thrown into eternal fire. And if your eye should cause you to sin, tear it out and throw it away: it is better for you to enter into life with one eye, than to have two eyes and be thrown into the hell of fire. See that you never despise any of these

little ones, for I tell you that their angels in heaven are continually in the presence of my Father in heaven."*(86)*

7. Lord, another point that particularly interested us in today's meditation was the fact that You reminded the Apostles of their pastoral responsibilities for those who strayed from You.

8. "Tell me. Suppose a man has a hundred sheep and one of them strays; will he not leave the ninety-nine on the hillside and go in search of the stray? I tell you solemnly, if he finds it, it gives him more joy than do the ninety-nine that did not stray at all. Similarly, it is never the will of your Father in heaven that one of these little ones should be lost."*(87)*

9. We learned from this, Lord, that Your "lost sheep" are to be charitably and constantly sought out, since they are of more immediate concern to You than those who have not lost Your friendship and grace.

10.   The responsibility for seeking the lost not only falls on the clergy, as some mistakenly suppose — but also upon Christian parents, teachers, friends, and others; all of whom are called to be their brother's keeper.

11.   Jesus, as You know better than anyone, Christians, even practicing Christians, do not always get along well with one another. Sometimes through misunderstanding, or even deliberate malice, a Christian pridefully accuses a fellow Christian of some misdeed, causing a rift to occur between them. Such a rift can be like the proverbial leak in the dike. It need not be long before deep resentment and even hatred arise, and other Christians may be asked to take sides. Before one realizes it, there is a flood of hatred and resentment to contend with. In the last analysis, this is advantageous only to satan and his followers.

12.   If one of our brothers in the Faith offends us, Lord, You tell us in effect to swallow our pride and be charitable towards him.

13.   " 'If your brother does something wrong, go and have it out with him alone, between your two selves. If he listens to you, you have won back your brother. If he does not listen, take one or two others along with you: the evidence of two or three witnesses is required to sustain any charge. But if he refuses to listen to these, report it to the community; and if he refuses to listen to the

community, treat him like a pagan or a tax collector.' "*(88)*

14.   Once a barrier has been established between two people, between two members of Your Church, You are telling us, Jesus, to approach our brother (or sister) privately, thereby avoiding embarrassment. If he listens and repents of his evil, his soul will be strengthened, and the offended one will have won back his brother. It is only when this gentle approach fails that sterner measures should be prayerfully taken.

15.   How often, Lord, we are guilty of failing to take constructive measures to overcome breaks in personal relationships. We tend to ignore solving such problems, hoping they will go away, or we attack them with an anger and zeal that are both unnecessary and counter-productive, thus causing even further divisions. You, on the other hand, tell us to take the approach which is both just and charitable.

16.   In today's meditation, Jesus, You teach us forgiveness. *(89)* When Peter asked how often he should forgive an offending brother, You answered him, "Seventy times seven." That is, an unending number of times. Then, Lord, You pointed out the necessary connection between Your forgiveness of our sins and our forgiveness of those who sin against us. If we do not from our hearts forgive those who offend us, neither will You forgive us. This is a very sobering thought, indeed, and entirely fair. ("As we forgive those who trespass against us . . .")

17.   Help us, Most Merciful Lord, always to forgive others when they offend us, even when they do not ask our forgiveness. By maintaining such an attitude, we are reflecting Your perfect charity in our lives. And for those who offend Your Most Sacred Heart through blasphemy, sacrilege and other offenses, inspire us to make acts of reparation for them. Amen. *(Reparation for sin is a term that many are not familiar with today. By it we help restore order in society by undoing the effects of sins. Therefore, the Apostolate is dedicated to promoting its practice as widely as possible. This goal was inspired by Pope Paul VI's document entitled "Indulgentiarum Doctrina" of January 1, 1967:*

18.   *"In fact, every sin upsets the universal order God, in His indescribable wisdom and limitless love, has established. Further, every sin does immense harm to the sinner himself and to the community of men.*

19.   *"The full taking away and, as it is called, reparation of sins requires two things. Firstly, friendship with God*

149

must be restored. Amends must be made for offending His wisdom and goodness. This is done by a sincere conversion of mind. Secondly, all the personal and social values, as well as those that are universal, which sin has lessened or destroyed must be fully made good.

20.   "By the hidden and kindly mystery of God's will a supernatural solidarity reigns among men. A consequence of this is that the sin of one person harms other people just as one person's holiness helps others.

21.   "This is the very ancient dogma called the Communion of Saints. It means that the life of each individual son of God is joined in Christ and through Christ by a wonderful link to the life of all his other Christian brethren. Together they form the supernatural unity of Christ's Mystical Body so that, as it were, a single mystical person is formed.

22.   "The 'treasury of the Church' is explained like this. We certainly should not think of it as being the sum total of the material goods which have accumulated during the

course of the centuries. On the contrary, the 'treasury of the Church' is the infinite value, which can never be exhausted, which Christ's merits have before God. They were offered so that the whole of mankind could be set free from sin and attain communion with the Father. In Christ, the Redeemer himself, the satisfactions and merits of His Redemption exist and find their efficacy. This treasury includes as well the prayers and good works of the Blessed Virgin Mary. They are truly immense, unfathomable and even pristine in their value before God. In the treasury, too, are the prayers and good works of all the saints, all those who have followed in the footsteps of Christ the Lord and by His grace have made their lives holy and carried out the mission of the Father entrusted to them. In this way they attained their own salvation and at the same time cooperated in saving their brothers in the unity of the Mystical Body.

23. "For these reasons a perennial link of charity exists between the faithful who have already reached their heavenly home (the Church Triumphant), those who are expiating their sins in purgatory (the Church Suffering) and those who are still pilgrims on earth (the Church Militant). Between them there is, too, an abundant exchange of all the goods by which divine justice is placated as expiation is made for all the sins of the whole of the Mystical Body. This is how God's mercy is led to forgiveness and it becomes possible for sinners who have repented sincerely, to share, as soon as they are capable of it, in the full enjoyment of the benefits of God's family."

Try to re-read and meditate on these Scripture passages and reflections at least one more time today.

Please refer to Chapter XIII, Paragraphs 1 to 17 of our "Peaceful Seed Living" prayer and meditation book, Volume II.

WEEK 2 DAY 6
The Gospel of St. Matthew
Chapter 19:1-30

VI. THE APPROACHING ADVENT OF THE KINGDOM OF HEAVEN

A. NARRATIVE SECTION

The question about divorce

1 **19**Jesus had now finished what he wanted to say, and he left Galilee and came into the part of Judaea which is on the far side 2 of the Jordan. ·Large crowds followed him and he healed them there.

3 Some Pharisees approached him, and to test him they said, "Is it against the Law for a man to divorce his wife on any pretext what-

4 ever?" •He answered, "Have you not read that the creator from the beginning *made*
5 *them male and female* •and that he said: *This is why a man must leave father and mother, and cling to his wife, and the two become one*
6 *body?* •They are no longer two, therefore, but one body. So then, what God has united, man must not divide." (C4) (C2)

7 They said to him, "Then why did Moses command that a writ of dismissal should be
8 given in cases of divorce?" •"It was because you were so unteachable," he said, "that Moses allowed you to divorce your wives, but it was not like this from the beginning. (C2)
9 Now I say this to you: the man who divorces his wife—I am not speaking of fornication —and marries another, is guilty of adultery." (C2)

Continence

10 The disciples said to him, "If that is how things are between husband and wife, it is not
11 advisable to marry." •But he replied, "It is not everyone who can accept what I have said, but only those to whom it is granted.
12 There are eunuchs born that way from their mother's womb, there are eunuchs made so by men and there are eunuchs who have made themselves that way for the sake of the kingdom of heaven. Let anyone accept this who can." (C3)

13 People brought little children to him, for (C3)
   him to lay his hands on them and say a prayer.
14 The disciples turned them away, ·but Jesus
   said, "Let the little children alone, and do not (C3)
   stop them coming to me; for it is to such as (C2)
   these that the kingdom of heaven belongs." (C3)
15 Then he laid his hands on them and went on (C3)
   his way.

The rich young man

16 And there was a man who came to him and
   asked, "Master, what good deed must I do
17 to possess eternal life?" ·Jesus said to him,
   "Why do you ask me about what is good?
   There is one alone who is good. But if you
   wish to enter into life, keep the command- (C3)
18 ments." ·He said, "Which?" "These:" Jesus
   replied *"You must not kill. You must not
   commit adultery. You must not steal. You* (C2)
19 *must not bring false witness.* · *Honor your fa-* (C3)
   ther and mother, and: *you must love your* (C3)
20 *neighbor as yourself."ᵃ* ·The young man said
   to him, "I have kept all these. What more do (C3)
21 I need to do?" ·Jesus said, "If you wish to
   be perfect, go and sell what you own and give (C3)
   the money to the poor, and you will have
   treasure in heaven; then come, follow me."
22 But when the young man heard these words (C2)
   he went away sad, for he was a man of great
   wealth.

The danger of riches

23 Then Jesus said to his disciples, "I tell you
   solemnly, it will be hard for a rich man to (C2)
24 enter the kingdom of heaven. ·Yes, I tell you
   again, it is easier for a camel to pass through
   the eye of a needle than for a rich man to
25 enter the kingdom of heaven." ·When the
   disciples heard this they were astonished.
26 "Who can be saved, then?" they said. ·Jesus
   gazed at them. "For men," he told them,

"this is impossible; for God everything is possible."

The reward of renunciation

27 Then Peter spoke. "What about us?" he (C1) said to him. "We have left everything and (C3) followed you. What are we to have, then?"

28 Jesus said to him, "I tell you solemnly, when all is made new and the Son of Man sits on his throne of glory, you will yourselves sit on twelve thrones to judge*b* the twelve tribes of

29 Israel. •And everyone who has left houses, (C1) brothers, sisters, father, mother, children or land for the sake of my name will be repaid (C3) a hundred times over, and also inherit eternal life.

30 "Many who are first will be last, and the (C4) last, first.

Week 2 Day 6
Four C's Meditations
on St. Matthew 19:1-30

1. Most Sacred Heart of Jesus, in today's reading St. Matthew once more presents us with Your teaching on the indissolubility or permanence of marriage. *(90)* Since this is so, and since there are so many factors today contributing to marital instability and divorce, how important it is for spouses to pray fervently for their marriages and to receive the sacraments often, so that they can be strengthened and purified by Your supernatural grace.

2. The grace of seed-charity is especially required. Just as fuel is necessary for the proper functioning of an automobile, so seed-charity is necessary for the proper functioning of a marriage. In the last analysis, it is the constant self-giving of each marital partner to the other, with the aid of Your grace, that will make a marriage work properly.

3. Thankfully, Lord, You also are a partner of every sacramental marriage. Consequently, Christian spouses can have the assurance that You would move mountains, if necessary, to make each and every Christian marriage work, as long as each and every husband and each and every wife cooperate with Your efforts. *(For a discussion of Matthew 19:9 see "The Catholic Catechism," pp. 356-358).*

4. Most kind and loving Savior, we noticed also in our Scripture reading that You addressed Yourself again to the subject of

small children. Here too, You stressed that it is to the child-like that the Kingdom of Heaven belongs.

5. "People brought little children to him, for him to lay his hands on them and say a prayer. The disciples turned them away, but Jesus said, 'Let the little children alone, and do not stop them coming to me; for it is to such as these that the kingdom of heaven belongs.' Then he laid his hands on them and went on his way." (91)

6. Jesus, may Your outstanding love for children always inspire us to follow Your example. We ask this particularly now because of the tendency among many married couples to place their own self-centered desires over the child-bearing and child-rearing duties of marriage. Consequently, there are more and more marriages in which the spouses deliberately choose not to have children. Moreover, even when there are children, there are increased instances of child neglect, including the unspeakable crime of abortion. And there are growing numbers of children scarred by the loss of their parents' mutual commitment to the life-long union of self-sacrificing love for one another.

7. Help us to understand Lord, that by our positive acts of reparation through fervent reception of the sacraments, prayer, sacrifices and example, we can protect the God-given rights of children everywhere, including their right to be born, their right to receive love

from each parent, and their right to witness the example of both parents sacrificially loving one another until death. Give us the grace not to pridefully judge but to pray with confidence that this generation will come to God and be abundantly blessed as Mary Magdalene was when she forsook her life of mortal sin. Let us not forget it is never too late for God's merciful forgiveness, and that we are to hate the sin but never the sinner. Moreover, constantly remind us that we are judged by God in the same measure we judge others.

8. Jesus, we also observed in today's meditation Your teaching on wealth.

9. "Then Jesus said to his disciples, 'I tell you solemnly, it will be hard for a rich man to enter the kingdom of heaven. Yes, I tell you again, it is easier for a camel to pass through the eye of a needle than for a rich man to enter the kingdom of heaven.' When the disciples heard this they were astonished.

'Who can be saved, then?' they said. Jesus gazed at them. 'For men,' he told them, 'this is impossible; for God everything is possible.'"*(92)*

10.   You imply here, Lord, that riches are a snare and a temptation for many, if not for most people. Certainly, wealth is not an evil in itself, but it is, nonetheless, easily abused, particularly by the greedy and by those who thirst to dominate the lives of others through their wealth. Moreover, even the poorest can seriously sin by their unholy desire to acquire wealth and by their envy of those who have more then they. Since this is so, help us to clearly understand it is not difficult to become so attached to riches and to *the pursuit of riches*, that we actually replace You as the One Whom we love first and foremost. This was true, for instance, in the case of St. Francis of Assisi who eventually renounced all of his wealth for the sake of his immortal soul. Could this not also possibly be the case with some of us? And can't we all be poor in spirit by being willing to give up everything rather than to betray You, O Lord?

11.   Jesus, Your advice to the rich young man in today's reading also reminds us that although wealth may not dominate our lives, it may be a hindrance to our growth in sanctity.*(93)* For that reason some of us who are not married might consider following Your recommendations and give up most, if not all, of our material possessions so we can focus our lives more on You and Your desire

159

for our holiness. In any case, we should be willing to give up everything before compromising Your will for us. *(Read "The Catholic Catechism," pp. 419-420 for some additional thoughts on this matter.)*

12. Jesus, there can be no doubt that a great many people today place too high a value on material possessions, trusting more in them than they do in You. Yet it is certain that riches cannot buy either lasting or "deep-down" happiness of soul, since only You can supply these. Nor should we forget that "The love of money is the root of all evil."*(94)* In other words, the love of money is simply a reflection of self-centeredness or pride, which leads to all other sins.

13. Lord, help us neither to despise nor crave wealth. Yet, for those of us who are well-off in a material sense, grant that we may always place You first in our lives and confide in You, Who give to all, rich and poor, the spiritual help we need in order to accomplish Your will in this life. Always remind us of our grave responsibilities in the use of our wealth, especially in helping the needy and poor.

14. Finally, Lord, we were struck by Peter's reminder that the Apostles had abandoned everything in order to follow You. You, in turn, assured him they would be rewarded for doing so, and that, indeed, everyone who gives up everything to follow You would be greatly compensated in this life and in the next. *(95)*

15. Most Sacred Heart of Jesus, You counsel some of us to abandon everything for the sake of promoting the Kingdom of Heaven on earth. For others, You seem to require it, as in the case of the Apostles themselves. But for still others, such as those with family responsibilities, it would be uncharitable for them to give up all their material possessions. But every Christian should be willing to abandon all of his material riches, if at some point in his life You clearly require or counsel it. Lord, may Your most loving will always be done on earth as it is in Heaven.

16. Jesus, Mary and Joseph, help us and all the members of our families and those of the

Apostolate to realize that only through a God-centered life can we find peace and true security. Amen.

Try to experience God's gift of peace, through the action of the Holy Spirit, by slowly re-reading and meditating on the Scripture for today.

Now you may refer to Chapter XIII, Paragraphs 18 to 40 of our "Peaceful Seed Living" prayer and meditation book, Volume II.

Parable of the vineyard laborers

20 1 "Now the kingdom of heaven is like a landowner going out at daybreak to 2 hire workers for his vineyard. ·He made an agreement with the workers for one denarius 3 a day, and sent them to his vineyard. ·Going out at about the third hour he saw others 4 standing idle in the market place ·and said to them, 'You go to my vineyard too and I will 5 give you a fair wage.' ·So they went. At about the sixth hour and again at about the ninth 6 hour, he went out and did the same. ·Then at about the eleventh hour he went out and found more men standing round, and he said to them, 'Why have you been standing here 7 idle all day?' ·'Because no one has hired us,' they answered. He said to them, 'You go into 8 my vineyard too.' ·In the evening, the owner of the vineyard said to his bailiff, 'Call the workers and pay them their wages, starting with the last arrivals and ending with the 9 first.' ·So those who were hired at about the eleventh hour came forward and received 10 one denarius each. ·When the first came, they expected to get more, but they too received 11 one denarius each. ·They took it, but grum-12 bled at the landowner. ·'The men who came last,' they said, 'have done only one hour, and you have treated them the same as us, though we have done a heavy day's work in all the 13 heat.' ·He answered one of them and said, 'My friend, I am not being unjust to you; did 14 we not agree on one denarius? ·Take your earnings and go. I choose to pay the last-15 comer as much as I pay you. ·Have I no right

to do what I like with my own? Why be envi- (C2)
16 ous because I am generous?' •Thus the last (C3)
will be first, and the first, last." (C4)

Third prophecy of the Passion

17 Jesus was going up to Jerusalem, and on
the way he took the Twelve to one side and
18 said to them, •"Now we are going up to
Jerusalem, and the Son of Man is about to
be handed over to the chief priests and (C2)
19 scribes. They will condemn him to death •and (C2)
will hand him over to the pagans to be (C2)
mocked and scourged and crucified; and on (C2)
the third day he will rise again."

The mother of Zebedee's sons makes her request

20 Then the mother of Zebedee's sons came
with her sons to make a request of him, and
21 bowed low; •and he said to her, "What is it
you want?" She said to him, "Promise that
these two sons of mine may sit one at your (C3)
right hand and the other at your left in your
22 kingdom." •"You do not know what you are
asking" Jesus answered. "Can you drink the
cup that I am going to drink?" They replied,
23 "We can." •"Very well," he said, "you shall (C3)

drink my cup,*a* but as for seats at my right hand and my left, these are not mine to grant; they belong to those to whom they have been allotted by my Father."

Leadership with service

24 When the other ten heard this they were
25 indignant with the two brothers. ·But Jesus called them to him and said, You know that among the pagans the rulers lord it over (C2) them, and their great men make their au-
26 thority felt. ·This is not to happen among you. (C2) No; anyone who wants to be great among you
27 must be your servant, ·and anyone who wants (C3) to be first among you must be your slave, (C3)
28 just as the Son of Man came not to be served but to serve, and to give his life as a ransom (C3) for many. '

The two blind men of Jericho

29 As they left Jericho a large crowd followed
30 him. ·Now there were two blind men sitting at the side of the road. When they heard that it was Jesus who was passing by, they shouted, "Lord! Have pity on us, Son of Da- (C1)
31 vid." ·And the crowd scolded them and told them to keep quiet, but they only shouted more loudly, "Lord! Have pity on us, Son of (C1)
32 David." ·Jesus stopped, called them over and said, "What do you want me to do for you?"
33 They said to him, "Lord, let us have our sight
34 back." ·Jesus felt pity for them and touched (C3) their eyes, and immediately their sight re- turned and they followed him. (C3)

The Messiah enters Jerusalem

1 **21** When they were near Jerusalem and had come in sight of Bethphage on the Mount of Olives, Jesus sent two disciples,
2 saying to them, "Go to the village facing you, and you will immediately find a tethered donkey and a colt with her. Untie them and

165

3 bring them to me. •If anyone says anything to you, you are to say, 'The Master needs them and will send them back directly.' "
4 This took place to fulfill the prophecy:

5 *Say to the daughter of Zion:*
Look, your king comes to you;
he is humble, he rides on a donkey
and on a colt, the foal of a beast of burden.ᵃ

6 So the disciples went out and did as Jesus had (C3)
7 told them. •They brought the donkey and the colt, then they laid their cloaks on their backs (C3)
8 and he sat on them. •Great crowds of people spread their cloaks on the road, while others (C3) were cutting branches from the trees and (C3)
9 spreading them in his path. •The crowds who went in front of him and those who followed were all shouting:

"Hosannaᵇ to the Son of David! (C3)
Blessings on him who comes in the name of the Lord!ᶜ
Hosanna in the highest heavens!" (C3)

10 And when he entered Jerusalem, the whole city was in turmoil. "Who is this?" people
11 asked, •and the crowds answered, "This is the prophet Jesus from Nazareth in Galilee."

166

12   Jesus then went into the Temple and drove
out all those who were selling and buying (C3)
there; he upset the tables of the money chang- (C2)
ers and the chairs of those who were selling
13 pigeons.*d* •"According to scripture," he said,
"my house will be called a house of prayer;e
but you are turning it into a *robbers' den."f* (C2)
14 There were also blind and lame people who
came to him in the Temple, and he cured (C3)
15 them. •At the sight of the wonderful things
he did and of the children shouting, "Hosanna to the Son of David," in the Temple, (C3)
the chief priests and the scribes were indig-
16 nant. •"Do you hear what they are saying?"
they said to him. "Yes," Jesus answered,
"have you never read this:

*By the mouths of children, babes in arms,
you have made sure of praise?"g*

17 With that he left them and went out of
the city to Bethany where he spent the
night.

The barren fig tree withers. Faith and prayer

18   As he was returning to the city in the early
19 morning, he felt hungry. •Seeing a fig tree by
the road, he went up to it and found nothing
on it but leaves. And he said to it, "May you
never bear fruit again"; and at that instant the
20 fig tree withered. •The disciples were amazed
when they saw it. "What happened to the
tree," they said, "that it withered there and
21 then?" •Jesus answered, "I tell you solemnly,
if you have faith and do not doubt at all, not (C1)
only will you do what I have done to the (C2)
fig tree, but even if you say to this mountain, 'Get up and throw yourself into the
22 sea,' it will be done. •And if you have faith, (C1)
everything you ask for in prayer you will receive."

167

23 He had gone into the Temple and was teaching, when the chief priests and the elders of the people came to him and said, "What authority have you for acting like this? 24 And who gave you this authority?" •"And I," replied Jesus, "will ask you a question, only one; if you tell me the answer to it, I will then tell you my authority for acting like this. 25 John's baptism: where did it come from: heaven or man?" And they argued it out this way among themselves, 'If we say from heaven, he will retort, 'Then why did you 26 refuse to believe him?'; •but if we say from man, we have the people to fear, for they all 27 hold that John was a prophet." •So their reply to Jesus was, "We do not know." And he retorted, "Nor will I tell you my authority for acting like this.

(C3)

(C2)

1. Most Sacred Heart of Jesus, Your parable about the vineyard workers especially caught our attention in today's meditation, since You reflected approval of what appeared to be an injustice.*(96)* We refer, of course, to the fact that all the workers received the same reward for their labors, although some worked longer and harder than others.

2. You were obviously making the point that salvation is available to all who love You, even though some love You more than others. Here You illustrate Your infinite love for all whom You admit to Your eternal Kingdom.

3. While in the last analysis, our salvation depends upon Your generosity, those who have received this free, unmerited, glorious gift do contribute to its retention and enhancement through their virtuous acts. Thus, the saints, because of their extraordinary good works on earth have increased their capacity to enjoy Your love to a greater degree in Heaven than do others who were not saints in this life, but who nevertheless died in Your friendship and were purified in Purgatory.

4. Jesus, help us always to keep in mind that in perfect justice You need not grant heavenly life to any human being. This is so

because the life of Your Kingdom is a sharing of Your own life which You are in no way bound to give to any creature.

5. On the other hand, Lord, it is very important for us to realize that our good works on earth, performed in Your friendship, do in fact, deserve a heavenly reward and contribute to the degree of bliss we will enjoy in the life to come. So we can say that although all the inhabitants of Heaven are there, because of Your generous love for them, the demands for justice are not ignored either. This can be seen, first of all, in the fact that all those who respond to Your love and persevere in it will be saved. Moreover, those who more perfectly cooperate with Your grace, i.e., work harder to fulfill Your commandments, will enjoy a greater measure of eternal happiness. In other words, their capacity to love You is made greater because of their greater sanctity.

6. Jesus, Mary and Joseph, help not only individuals, as such, but also families to strive daily for sanctity by sowing seeds of charity among themselves so that each and every family member may not lose Your free gift of eternal life.

7. Lord, we also noted with admiration in today's meditation the willingness of the Apostles James and John to share in drinking the bitter cup of Your Passion, i.e., Your suffering. Clearly, they possessed the spirit of seed-charity and constancy. *(97)*

8. Moreover, St. Paul tells us that every Christian must suffer for Your Name's sake if he is to enter Your Kingdom.

9. "You are well aware, then, that anybody who tries to live in devotion to Christ is certain to be attacked." "We all have to experience many hardships...before we enter the Kingdom of God." *(98)*

10. St. Peter even writes that we should be glad when we suffer on Your account.

11. "If you have some share in the sufferings of Christ, be glad, because you will enjoy a much greater gladness when his glory is revealed." *(99)*

12. And we share in Your suffering, Lord, when, for example, we resist sinful temptation. This type of suffering always reflects our love for You and it is necessary for us to accept it. There are other types of suffering and sacrifices, however, as You well know,

171

which we can accept for a greater advancement of Your Kingdom but are not, strictly speaking, required of us. Thus, we can voluntarily give up some earthly goods or some innocent pleasure. Or we can accept work that pays little and demands much, but offers the opportunity for doing a great amount of good. Or we can earn indulgences for the Poor Souls in Purgatory. Help us, Lord, to realize that this type of suffering is especially pleasing to You, and those who freely accept it will be generously rewarded in this life and in the next. *(For a discussion of Christian generosity, see "The Catholic Catechism." pp. 430-432. Read also pp. 560-570 for information on indulgences.)*

13. In today's reading, Jesus, You also pointed out the importance of serving others.

14. "But Jesus called them to him and said, 'You know that among the pagans the ruler lords it over them, and their great men make their authority felt. This is not to happen

among you. No; anyone who wants to be great among you must be your servant, and anyone who wants to be first among you must be your slave, just as the Son of Man came not to be served but to serve, and to give his life as a ransom for many.' " *(100)*

15.   We learned from this, Lord, that the degree of our sanctity has a direct relationship to the degree we serve others. *(101)* Moreover, when we serve others sacrificially we are serving You as well. Also, You rightly used Yourself as the prime example of what it means to serve others. Thus You, Who are God, humbled Yourself to take on our human nature. Not only that, but You humbled Yourself even further by Your life of complete surrender to the will of the Father, even to the point of freely accepting Your horrible death on the Cross so that our redemption could be obtained. What a contrast is seen here between what constitutes Christian greatness and the greatness sought after by worldly souls.

16.   We praise and thank You, Jesus, for being our Suffering Servant. May we follow in Your footsteps and thus enter Your Kingdom. And when we strive to serve others, help us first of all to serve the God-given needs of our families. *(The title "Suffering Servant" was used by the Old Testament prophet Isaiah with reference to the future Messiah. See, e.g., Isaiah ch. 53.)*

17.   In chapter twenty-one of our meditation, Most Merciful Savior, St.

173

Matthew tells us the story of the crowds who praised You, shouting, "Hosanna to the Son of David! Hosanna in the highest heaven."(102) This act of praise was a reflection of the charity that the masses of ordinary people held for You.

18. On account of Your infinite goodness and mercy towards us, Lord, it is only right that we should praise You gladly and often in prayers and in worship. Nonetheless, there is a tendency for many of us to pray only for our needs and for the needs of others. Consequently, may Your Holy Spirit inspire us to also praise and thank You often both in our daily prayers and at Mass.

19. Most Sacred Heart of Jesus, in today's meditation, we noticed after You caused the fig tree to wither, You once more stressed the importance of the supernatural virtue of faith.

20. "I tell you solemnly, if you have faith and do not doubt at all, not only will you do what I have done to the fig tree, but even if you say to this mountain, 'Get up and throw yourself into the sea,' it will be done. And if you have faith, everything you ask for in prayer you will receive."*(103)*

21. Lord, in this instance You were preparing Your disciples for the time when You would no longer be with them in Your visible body. The time would come when You would be only present invisibly. Thus to believe in Your invisible presence, great faith and trust would be required, and You would choose prayer as the means to communicate with You. This, of course, is true for us also, and the greater our faith and trust in You when we pray, the more effective our prayers will be. Once more, we ask You to give us the faith (and trust) that can move mountains so that we may serve You and others better.

22. Most Holy Family, inspire us and the members of our families as well as the members and friends of the Apostolate to maintain a positive and expecting attitude throughout our lifetime. Also unite our prayers with all the other members of the Apostolate throughout the world and place us in the Eucharistic presence of Jesus in our parish churches, and in the Apostolate's Sacred Hearts Chapel at The House of St. Joseph. Help us, most of all, to remember that we are living in Your presence every day

and should persevere by looking for Your
answers in both great events and small. Amen.

*Try to read these Scripture passages and meditations
more than once a day in a reflective manner. Many
families read them first together and then a second time
individually. You and your family might find this helpful
also. Each time you do so, the Holy Spirit will give you
more insights.*

*Please reflectively read Chapter XIV, Paragraphs 1 to 9
and Chapter XV, Paragraphs 1 and 2 of our "Peaceful
Seed Living" prayer and meditation book, Volume II.*

Parable of the two sons

28 "What is your opinion? A man had two
sons. He went and said to the first, 'My boy,
29 you go and work in the vineyard today.' ·He
answered, 'I will not go,' but afterwards (C2)
30 thought better of it and went. ·The man then (C3)
went and said the same thing to the second
who answered, 'Certainly, sir,' but did not go. (C2)
31 Which of the two did the father's will?" "The
first," they said. Jesus said to them, "I tell you
solemnly, tax collectors and prostitutes are
making their way into the kingdom of God (C3)
32 before you. ·For John came to you, a pattern (C3)
of true righteousness, but you did not believe (C2)
him, and yet the tax collectors and prostitutes
did. Even after seeing that, you refused to (C1)
think better of it and believe in him. (C1)
(C2)

Parable of the wicked husbandmen

33 "Listen to another parable. There was a
man, a landowner, who planted a vineyard;
he fenced it round, dug a winepress in it and
built a tower; then he leased it to tenants and
34 went abroad. ·When vintage time drew near
he sent his servants to the tenants to collect
35 his produce. ·But the tenants seized his serv- (C2)
ants, thrashed one, killed another and stoned
36 a third. ·Next he sent some more servants,
this time a larger number, and they dealt with
37 them in the same way. ·Finally he sent his son (C2)
to them. 'They will respect my son,' he said.
38 But when the tenants saw the son, they said
to each other, 'This is the heir. Come on, let
us kill him and take over his inheritance.'
39 So they seized him and threw him out of the (C2)

177

40 vineyard and killed him. ·Now when the owner of the vineyard comes, what will he

41 do to those tenants?" ·They answered, "He will bring those wretches to a wretched end (C2) and lease the vineyard to other tenants who will deliver the produce to him when the sea-

42 son arrives." ·Jesus said to them, "Have you never read in the scriptures:

> *It was the stone rejected by the builders* (C2)
> *that became the keystone.*
> *This was the Lord's doing*
> *and it is wonderful to see?*[h]

43 I tell you, then, that the kingdom of God will be taken from you and given to a people who will produce its fruit." (C3)

45 When they heard his parables, the chief priests and the scribes realized he was speak-

46 ing about them, ·but though they would have liked to arrest him they were afraid of the (C2) crowds, who looked on him as a prophet.

1
2 **22** Jesus began to speak to them in parables once again, •"The kingdom of
heaven may be compared to a king who gave
3 a feast for his son's wedding. •He sent his
servants to call those who had been invited,
4 but they would not come. •Next he sent some
more servants. 'Tell those who have been
invited,' he said, 'that I have my banquet all
prepared, my oxen and fattened cattle have
been slaughtered, everything is ready. Come
5 to the wedding.' •But they were not interested: one went off to his farm, another to his
6 business, •and the rest seized his servants, (C2)
7 maltreated them and killed them. •The king (C2)
was furious. He despatched his troops, destroyed those murderers and burned their
8 town. •Then he said to his servants, 'The
wedding is ready; but as those who were in-
9 vited proved to be unworthy, •go to the cross- (C2)
roads in the town and invite everyone you can
10 find to the wedding.' •So these servants went (C3)
out on to the roads and collected together
everyone they could find, bad and good alike;
and the wedding hall was filled with guests.
11 When the king came in to look at the guests
he noticed one man who was not wearing a
12 wedding garment, •and said to him, 'How did (C2)
you get in here, my friend, without a wedding (C2)
13 garment?" And the man was silent. •Then the
king said to the attendants, 'Bind him hand
and foot and throw him out into the dark,
where there will be weeping and grinding of
14 teeth.' •For many are called, but few are (C3)
chosen." (C2)

On tribute to Caesar

15   Then the Pharisees went away to work out
between them how to trap him in what he (C2)
16 said. •And they sent their disciples to him,
together with the Herodians,*a* to say, "Master, we know that you are an honest man and

teach the way of God in an honest way, and
that you are not afraid of anyone, because a
17 man's rank means nothing to you. •Tell us
your opinion, then. Is it permissible to pay
18 taxes to Caesar or not?" •But Jesus was
aware of their malice and replied, "You hypo- (C2)
19 crites! Why do you set this trap for me? •Let (C2)
me see the money you pay the tax with."
20 They handed him a denarius, •and he said,
21 "Whose head is this? Whose name?" •"Caesar's," they replied. He then said to them,
"Very well, give back to Caesar what belongs
to Caesar—and to God what belongs to (C3)
22 God." •This reply took them by surprise, and
they left him alone and went away.

The resurrection of the dead

23   That day some Sadducees—who deny that
there is a resurrection—approached him and
24 they put this question to him, •"Master,
Moses said that if a man dies childless, his
brother is to marry the widow, his sister-in-
25 law, to raise children for his brother. •Now
we had a case involving seven brothers; the
first married and then died without children,
26 leaving his wife to his brother; •the same
thing happened with the second and third and

27 so on to the seventh, •and then last of all the
28 woman herself died. •Now at the resurrection
to which of those seven will she be wife,
since she had been married to them all?"
29 Jesus answered them, "You are wrong, because you understand neither the scriptures
30 nor the power of God. •For at the resurrection men and women do not marry; no, they
31 are like the angels in heaven. •And as for
the resurrection of the dead, have you never
32 read what God himself said to you: •*I am the
God of Abraham, the God of Isaac and the
God of Jacob?b* God is God, not of the dead,
33 but of the living." •And his teaching made a
deep impression on the people who heard
it.

The greatest commandment of all

34   But when the Pharisees heard that he had
silenced the Sadducees they got together
35 and, to disconcert him, one of them put a   (C2)
36 question, •"Master, which is the greatest
37 commandment of the Law?" •Jesus said,
"You must love the Lord your God with all   (C3)
your heart, with all your soul, and with all
38 your mind. •This is the greatest and the first
39 commandment. •The second resembles it: (C3)
40 *You must love your neighbor as yourself.* •On
these two commandments hang the whole
Law, and the Prophets also."

Christ not only son but also Lord of David

41   While the Pharisees were gathered round,
42 Jesus put to them this question, •"What is
your opinion about the Christ? Whose son is
43 he?" "David's," they told him. •"Then how
is it," he said, "that David, moved by the
Spirit, calls him Lord, where he says:

44   *The Lord said to my Lord:*
Sit at my right hand
and I will put your enemies   (C2)
under your feet?c

181

45 "If David can call him Lord, then how can
46 he be his son?" ·Not one could think of anything to say in reply, and from that day no
one dared to ask him any further questions.

Week 3 Day 1
Four C's Meditations
on St. Matthew 21:28-22:46

1.   Most Merciful Savior, Your parable of the
two sons — the one obedient, the other
disobedient — clearly has a bearing on family
life today. (104) It is not at all uncommon to see
these two reflected in so many of our families.
Some children often balk at the thought of the
work that their parents or others in authority
require of them. They even go so far as to say
they will not do it. Yet, many of these same
children, after giving the matter further
thought, repent of their disobedience and,
with unselfish love, do what they were told to
do. There are other children, however, who

say they will do what is required of them, yet fail to do it. These, then, earn the displeasure of their parents or others who are in charge of them.

2. From another point of view, Lord, the parable points to all who deliberately follow their own will rather than Yours; to those who, in effect say, "No", to You. But You in Your wonderful providence never tire of inspiring them to purify their consciences through repentance and to exercise charity by choosing the good. Consequently, many have repented and turned to You, accepting the primacy of Your will in their lives. But there are others, who on the surface, at least, claim they obey You but lack the supernatural gift of seed-charity. These do not openly lead scandalous lives. They may attend Mass weekly, or give to the poor and needy, and do other things that are good in themselves. Yet, inwardly, they are disobedient since they are mainly motivated by their will rather than Yours. Some refer to this attitude as "enlightened self-interest."

3. St. Paul speaks of such selfishness in the following words:

4. "If I have all the eloquence of men or of angels, but speak without love (seed-charity), I am simply a gong booming or a cymbal clashing. If I have the gift of prophecy, understanding all the mysteries there are, knowing everything, and if I have faith in all its fullness, to move mountains, but without love (seed-charity) then I am nothing at all. If I give away

all that I possess, piece by piece, if I even let them take my body to burn it, but am without love (seed-charity), it will do me no good whatever." *(105)*

5.   Dear Lord, help us who outwardly lead respectable lives to conform inwardly to Your will which alone brings true peace and contentment.

6.   The Parable of the Wicked Landowner in today's reading, Jesus, reminds us of those who call themselves Catholics, yet refuse to accept Your Church's doctrine in its entirety. *(106)* Their lives, given to them by You, are meant to be cared for and nourished with the assistance of the teachings of Your Catholic Church. Yet, they reject those who seek to convey many of these truths to them, whether those who teach them are parents, pastors, teachers or bishops. They do not hesitate to reject even Your Vicar on earth, the Holy Roman Pontiff.

7.   Lord, grant that we may always accept the fullness of Your teachings as taught by the Holy Roman Catholic Church, and enable us to put them into practice motivated by seed-charity. We pray also for those who refuse to accept all of Your doctrine. By means of our prayers and good examples, may they receive the totality of Your saving light and enjoy the comfort and peace of Your presence.

8.   The Parable of the Wedding Feast brings to mind, O Lord, those of us whom You have called to salvation, yet are so occupied with life in the material world that we fail to reflect sufficiently on spiritual realities, such as Yourself and Your will for us.*(107)* Far too many of us fail to find time for You Who are the Source of our lives and our well-being. Obviously, when we fall into this trap we do not exercise faith in You, nor do we perform grace-filled works of sacrificial love which lead to holiness and eternal salvation.

9.   Lord help all of us, through Your grace, to never think we are so busy that we must neglect our prayer life and not place You first in our lives. Inspire us to repent of our erroneous paths and to turn to You. Help us say the right things to others so they might more readily discover Your loving presence in their midst. Jesus, also help those who consciously try to do Your will, so they will not become so involved in worldly things, such as their recreation, jobs and politics, that they forget You Who are the true Center of all

reality and the only One Who can give them everlasting happiness and joy.

10.   Lord Jesus, our eyes focused in our meditation on the greatest of Your commandments which states we are to love You and the Father and the Holy Spirit first and foremost with our whole being, and secondly, we are to love all our fellow humans as we love ourselves. *(108)* This commandment would be impossible to keep, if it weren't for Your gift of seed-charity. Thank You, Lord, for earning and providing it for us.

11.   When we love You and the Father and the Holy Spirit above all things we are putting things in their proper perspective since You as God are the Center of reality and the Source of all good things, including our happiness and our peace and our joy. When we love You first and foremost, we are then able to love ourselves as we ought and to love all others as ourselves.

186

12.   In St. John's Gospel, You clarify what You mean by loving others. Jesus, You said we are to love them as You have loved us. *(109)* How then did You love us? And how do You love us now? The answer, of course, is with seed-charity. That is, with love that is not selfish but seeks what is best for us. Basically then, this means we are to love others with the view of helping them obtain and keep salvation.

13.   Lord, grant us daily to increase in seed-charity and to use it for Your honor and glory and for the salvation of others, including the salvation of our enemies as You have commanded us to do. *(110)*

14.   Most Holy Family, inspire us to take advantage of our daily opportunities to plant seeds of charity, that is, to sacrifice ourselves for others and to pray for them. But especially inspire us to freely give of our prayers, our time, and our compassion to the members of our own families, and also to others living and working near us, each of whom is a temple of the Holy Spirit. Amen.

The more you re-read these Scriptures and meditations, the more you will get out of them.

Please refer to Chapter XVI, Paragraphs 1-9; XVII, Paragraphs 1 to 2; and XVIII, Paragraphs 1-4 of our "Peaceful Seed Living" prayer and meditation book, Volume II.

The scribes and Pharisees: their hypocrisy and vanity

23 ¹Then addressing the people and his disciples Jesus said, •²"The scribes and the Pharisees occupy the chair of Moses. •You ³must therefore do what they tell you and listen to what they say; but do not be guided by what they do: since they do not practice what they preach. •⁴They tie up heavy burdens and lay them on men's shoulders, but will they lift a finger to move them? Not they! •⁵Everything they do is done to attract attention, like wearing broader phylacteries and ⁶longer tassels,ᵃ •like wanting to take the place of honor at banquets and the front seats in ⁷the synagogues, •being greeted obsequiously in the market squares and having people call them Rabbi. (C3) (C1) (C2) (C2) (C2) (C2) (C2) (C2) (C2)

188

8   "You, however, must not allow yourselves
to be called Rabbi, since you have only one
9 Master, and you are all brothers. ·You must
call no one on earth your father, since you
have only one Father, and he is in heaven.
10 Nor must you allow yourselves to be called
teachers, for you have only one Teacher, the
11 Christ. ·The greatest among you must be   (C3)
12 your servant. ·Anyone who exalts himself   (C2)
will be humbled, and anyone who humbles   (C3)
himself will be exalted.

The sevenfold indictment of the scribes and Pharisees

13   "Alas for you, scribes and Pharisees, you   (C2)
hypocrites! You who shut up the kingdom of
heaven in men's faces, neither going in your-   (C2)
selves nor allowing others to go in[b] who want   (C3)
14 to.[c]
15   "Alas for you, scribes and Pharisees, you   (C2)
hypocrites! You who travel over sea and land
to make a single proselyte, and when you
have him you make him twice as fit for hell   (C2)
as you are.
16   "Alas for you, blind guides! You who say,   (C2)
'If a man swears by the Temple, it has no
force; but if a man swears by the gold of the
17 Temple, he is bound.' ·Fools and blind! For   (C2)
which is of greater worth, the gold or the
18 Temple that makes the gold sacred? ·Or else,
'If a man swears by the altar it has no force;
but if a man swears by the offering that is on
19 the altar, he is bound.' ·You blind men! For   (C2)
which is of greater worth, the offering or the
20 altar that makes the offering sacred? ·There-
fore, when a man swears by the altar he is
21 swearing by that and by everything on it.·And
when a man swears by the Temple he is
swearing by that and by the One who dwells
22 in it. ·And when a man swears by heaven he
is swearing by the throne of God and by the
One who is seated there.
23   "Alas for you, scribes and Pharisees, you   (C2)
hypocrites! You who pay your tithe of mint

189

and dill and cummin^d and have neglected (C2)
the weightier matters of the Law—justice, (C3)
mercy, good faith! These you should have
practiced, without neglecting the others. (C2)
24 You blind guides! Straining out gnats and (C2)
swallowing camels!

25 "Alas for you, scribes and Pharisees, you
hypocrites! You who clean the outside of cup (C2)
and dish and leave the inside full of extortion (C2)
26 and intemperance. •Blind Pharisee! Clean the (C2)
inside of cup and dish first so that the outside
may become clean as well.

27 "Alas for you, scribes and Pharisees, you
hypocrites! You who are like whitewashed (C2)
tombs that look handsome on the outside, but
inside are full of dead men's bones and every
28 kind of corruption. •In the same way you
appear to people from the outside like good
honest men, but inside you are full of hypoc- (C2)
risy and lawlessness.

29 "Alas for you, scribes and Pharisees, you
hypocrites! You who build the sepulchres of (C2)
the prophets and decorate the tombs of holy
30 men, •saying, 'We would never have joined
in shedding the blood of the prophets, had
31 we lived in our fathers' day.' •So! Your own (C2)
evidence tells against you! You are the sons (C2)
32 of those who murdered the prophets! •Very (C2)
well then, finish off the work that your fathers
began.

33 "Serpents, brood of vipers, how can you
34 escape being condemned to hell? •This is (C2)
    why, in my turn, I am sending you prophets
    and wise men and scribes: some you will
    slaughter and crucify, some you will scourge (C2)
    in your synagogues and hunt from town to
35 town; •and so you will draw down on your-
    selves the blood of every holy man that has
    been shed on earth, from the blood of Abel
    the Holy to the blood of Zechariah son of
    Barachiah*c* whom you murdered between the (C2)
36 sanctuary and the altar. •I tell you solemnly,
    all of this will recoil on this generation.

Jerusalem admonished

37 "Jerusalem, Jerusalem, you that kill the (C2)
    prophets and stone those who are sent to you!
    How often have I longed to gather your chil- (C3)
    dren, as a hen gathers her chicks under her (C3)
38 wings, and you refused! •So be it! Your house
39 will be left to you desolate, •for, I promise,
    you shall not see me any more until you
    say:

*Blessings on him who comes in the name of
    the Lord!f*

191

Week 3 Day 2
Four C's Meditations
on St. Matthew 23:1-39

1. In today's Scripture reading, Lord Jesus, You once more spoke disapprovingly of the Pharisees. You did this so often because the Pharisees were religious leaders, whom people respected and followed. Many of the Pharisees appeared to be holy, God-fearing, charitable men but, in fact, were fundamentally self-centered, leading many astray.

2. A person who is a notorious criminal, or who deliberately leads an openly scandalous life, is clearly seen for what he is and his company is shunned by those who wish to do God's will. But one who is a religious leader, outwardly holy, yet in reality a hypocrite, may not be so easily detected for the person he actually is. Thus, those who looked to the Pharisees, as a group, for spiritual guidance were in fact seeking help from wolves in sheep's clothing.

3. What is even worse is the fact that many who detected the hypocrisy of the Pharisees were undoubtedly tempted to conclude that the religion the Pharisees represented was false, and therefore they were tempted to reject it.

4. With this in mind, Lord, help Christians in positions of spiritual authority, such as parents and clergy, to avoid every semblance of hypocrisy so they will never lead anyone down the path of perdition.

5.   Most Sacred Heart of Jesus, we noted, too, that You told Your hearers that the Pharisees (and scribes), as the official teachers of Moses' doctrine, were to be listened to. But when it came to modeling one's life on these men, You said this was not to be done since their practice did not reflect Moses' teachings.

6.   You also pointed out that the Pharisees sometimes deliberately misinterpreted the Law of Moses. They also attracted undue attention to themselves and fostered their own well-being rather than the glory and honor of Your heavenly Father. *(111)*

7.   Lord, because we too are prone to sin, we earnestly ask You to help us avoid all sins, but particularly to avoid the sin of hypocrisy. May our lives constantly reflect the virtuous seed-charity and humility which You perfectly exemplified while on earth. May we not be primarily concerned with keeping only the let-

ter of Your commandments, but rather with observing their spirit, which consists in the sacrifice of one's self in generous love for God and for others. And may those in positions of spiritual leadership, including parents, continually remember the great responsibility they have for setting a holy example for all whom You have called to serve in Your Name.

8. Also, Lord, in today's reading it was again evident the scribes and Pharisees were completely blind to the fact You were the long-awaited Messiah. This was the case in spite of the fact they experienced Your holiness of life, the soundness of Your doctrine and the many miracles You performed. Not only did their hardness of heart produce spiritual blindness as to Who You were, they were even convinced You were a false prophet inspired by satan and deserving of death. Moreover, their hypocrisy was particularly glaring when they affirmed that had they been alive when their fathers were they would never have murdered God's prophets. *(112)*

9. Lord, this serves to remind us that we must always be open to recognizing those who are Your authentic representatives in the Church. Certainly, every priest, when he celebrates the sacraments according to the norms prescribed by the Church, represents You faithfully by being Your instrument of saving grace. And those are Your true representatives, as well, who teach as necessary for salvation only the doctrines upheld by the Church of Rome. But those who, not only teach in Your Name, but also consistently

practice acts of faith, hope and seed-charity are the ones who most deserve our fullest support and sympathy. Unfortunately, they are often subjected to ridicule and opposition, even as You were. Lord, help us to always recognize these saintly servants of Yours and help us to model our lives after them.

10. Finally, Jesus, we noticed in our meditation Your great love for the city of Jerusalem.(113) Just as You loved the old Jerusalem, so You now love Your Church which is the New Jerusalem, the Mother of us all.(114) It is Your own Mystical Body which You always nourish and feed through the Holy Sacrifice of the Mass. May we, who help constitute Your Mystical Body, always realize the importance and great benefits we receive from frequent Holy Communion and participation in the Eucharistic Sacrifice, benefits which enable us to serve You as seeds of charity for the advancement of Your heavenly Kingdom. Amen.

(For more information on the Church as Christ's Mystical Body, see pp. 210-211 of "The Catholic Catechism.")
Try to read these Scripture passages and meditations in a reflective manner at least one more time today. The Holy Spirit will reveal more insights to you each time you do so. Please refer to Chapter XIX, Paragraphs 1 to 21 of our "Peaceful Seed Living" prayer and meditation book, Volume II.

B. THE SERMON ON THE END

Introduction

1 **24** Jesus left the Temple, and as he was going away his disciples came up to draw his attention to the Temple buildings. 2 He said to them in reply, "You see all these? I tell you solemnly, not a single stone here will be left on another: everything will be 3 destroyed." ·And when he was sitting on the Mount of Olives the disciples came and asked him privately, "Tell us, when is this going to happen, and what will be the sign of your coming and of the end of the world?"

4 And Jesus answered them, "Take care that [C3]
5 no one deceives you; ·because many will [C2]
come using my name and saying, 'I am the [C2]
6 Christ,' and they will deceive many. ·You will
hear of wars and rumors of wars; do not be
alarmed, for this is something that must hap-
7 pen, but the end will not be yet. ·For nation
will fight against nation, and kingdom against [C2]
kingdom. There will be famines and earth-
8 quakes here and there. ·All this is only the
beginning of the birthpangs.

9 "Then they will hand you over to be tor- [C2]
tured and put to death; and you will be hated [C2]
by all the nations on account of my name.
10 And then many will fall away; men will betray [C2]
11 one another and hate one another. ·Many [C2]
false prophets will arise; they will deceive [C2]
12 many, ·and with the increase of lawlessness,
13 love in most men will grow cold; ·but the man [C2]
who stands firm to the end will be saved. [C4]
14 "This Good News of the kingdom will be [C3]
proclaimed to the whole world[a] as a witness
to all the nations. And then the end[b] will
come.

The great tribulation of Jerusalem

15 "So when you see *the disastrous abomina-
tion,* of which the prophet Daniel spoke, set [C2]
up in the Holy Place (let the reader under-
16 stand), ·then those in Judaea must escape to
17 the mountains; ·if a man is on the housetop,
he must not come down to collect his belong-
18 ings; ·if a man is in the fields, he must not
19 turn back to fetch his cloak. ·Alas for those
with child, or with babies at the breast, when
20 those days come! ·Pray that you will not have [C1]
21 to escape in winter or on a sabbath. ·For then
there will be *great distress such as, until now,* [C2]
since the world began, there never *has been,*
22 nor ever will be again. ·And if that time had

197

not been shortened, no one would have sur-
vived; but shortened that time shall be, for the
sake of those who are chosen.

23 "If anyone says to you then, 'Look, here
is the Christ,' or, 'He is there,' do not believe
24 it; ·for false Christs and false prophets will (C2)
arise and produce great signs and portents,
enough to deceive even the chosen, if that
25 were possible. ·There; I have forewarned (C3)
you.

The coming of the Son of Man will be evident

26 "If, then, they say to you, 'Look, he is in
the desert,' do not go there; 'Look, he is in
27 some hiding place,' do not believe it; ·be-
cause the coming of the Son of Man will be
like lightning striking in the east and flashing
28 far into the west. ·Wherever the corpse is,
there will the vultures gather.

The universal significance of this coming

29 "Immediately after the distress of those
days*c* the sun will be darkened, the moon will
lose its brightness, the stars will fall from the
sky and the powers of heaven will be shaken.
30 And then the sign of the Son of Man will
appear in heaven; then too all the peoples of

the earth will beat their breasts; and they will
see the Son of Man coming on the clouds of
31 heaven with power and great glory.*d* •And he
will send his angels with a loud trumpet to
gather his chosen from the four winds, from   (C3)
one end of heaven to the other.   (C4)

The time of this coming

32 "Take the fig tree as a parable: as soon as
its twigs grow supple and its leaves come out,
33 you know that summer is near. •So with you
when you see all these things: know that he
34 is near, at the very gates. •I tell you solemnly,
before this generation has passed away all
35 these things will have taken place.*e* •Heaven
and earth will pass away, but my words will
36 never pass away. •But as for that day and
hour, nobody knows it, neither the angels of
heaven, nor the Son, no one but the Father
only.

Be on the alert

37 "As it was in Noah's day, so will it be when
38 the Son of Man comes. •For in those days
before the Flood people were eating, drinking, taking wives, taking husbands, right up
39 to the day Noah went into the ark, •and they
suspected nothing till the Flood came and
swept all away. It will be like this when the
40 Son of Man comes. •Then of two men in the   (C2)
41 fields one is taken, one left; •of two women   (C3)
at the millstone grinding, one is taken, one
left.

42 "So stay awake, because you do not know   (C4)
43 the day when your master is coming. •You   (C1)
may be quite sure of this that if the   (C3)
householder had known at what time of the
night the burglar would come, he would have   (C2)
stayed awake and would not have allowed   (C4)
anyone to break through the wall of his   (C5)
44 house. •Therefore, you too must stand ready

because the Son of Man is coming at an hour you do not expect.

Parable of the conscientious steward

45 "What sort of servant, then, is faithful and (C3) wise enough for the master to place him over his household to give them their food at the
46 proper time? •Happy that servant if his master's arrival finds him at this employment. (C3) (C4)
47 I tell you solemnly, he will place him over
48 everything he owns. •But as for the dishonest (C2) servant who says to himself, 'My master is
49 taking his time,' •and sets about beating his (C2) fellow servants and eating and drinking with (C2)
50 drunkards, •his master will come on a day he does not expect and at an hour he does not
51 know. •The master will cut him off and send him to the same fate as the hypocrites, where (C2) there will be weeping and grinding of teeth.

200

Week 3 Day 3
Four C's Meditations
on St. Matthew 24:1-51

1. Jesus, Our Lord and Our Savior, in today's Scripture reading, You spoke of the impending destruction of the holy Temple in Jerusalem.*(115)* We also learned of Your instructions to the disciples in which You prepared them for the time of great tribulation which would signal the end of the Old Testament period and the beginning of the messianic era, the era of the New Testament, which would be open, not only to the Jews, but to all peoples and nations.*(116)*

2. Lord, while speaking to the disciples about these things, You implied the need for constant faith and trust in You, as well as the possession of constant charity, since temptations to turn from You and Your Gospel would be great. Specifically, You noted that among Your followers, some would be tortured and killed, and others would fall away. Also, You said divisions among Christians would occur, and the spirit of generous self-giving would grow cold. Yet those who remained steadfast in faith and hope, keeping themselves free from sin and performing acts of sacrificial love would be saved.

3. Lord, these words of Yours also have meaning for us today. Temptations to depart from You and Your doctrines face us daily. Atheism, agnosticism, scepticism, laxity in morals, self-indulgence, lack of piety, and irreverence for all things holy, seem to be

everywhere. Help us not to disregard those practices of our Faith which we find hard to follow. Moreover, when we recall Your words, "By their fruits you shall know them," *(117)* we think, among other things, of the evil fruits of abortion, greed and immoral sexual conduct, which are so commonplace today.

4. Lord, instead of giving in to the allurements of sin, help us always to follow Your saints who bore super-abundant spiritual fruit in this life. And may the power of their intercession enable us to remain steadfast in our vocation as Christians and faithfully serve You and others until our life's end.

5. Jesus, You warned Your disciples that many false prophets would arise before the destruction of Jerusalem and the Temple, and indeed they did. *(118)* False prophets are also with us now. We mean those who claim to represent You, but in fact do not. They can

be recognized by their fruit, especially the fruit of their false doctrine, which fails to reflect the teaching of the Church of Rome.

6. Lord, help us always to be on our guard against false doctrine and accept only that which Your Vicar, the Roman Pontiff, teaches or approves. In him we can have confidence, because in matters of faith and morals he can never deceive nor be deceived.

7. You also described in today's reading, Lord, what would happen at Your Second Coming at the end of the world. *(119)* The number who will lack constancy in charity at that time will be great. Therefore, You stressed the necessity of constant vigilance in order to prepare for Your Coming. Those who fail to be vigilant will be denied access to Your everlasting Kingdom and will weep and "grind their teeth." *(120) (Some scholars believe Jesus' words here also applied to the destruction of Jerusalem in A.D. 70.)*

8. Although, we who are alive now may not be here on earth when You return again in glory, we most certainly will face You either as Friend or Foe when we die. In the meantime, sin is always with us and we must never presume that we will persevere in doing Your will until either the world ends or until the moment of our death. The man left in the field at Your Coming, the woman left at the mill, and the dishonest servant serve as a warning for us, Lord.

9. We must not let down our guard. Our end on earth can occur at any time. We must

remain vigilant in the practice of our Faith. Fervent prayer and the fervent reception of the sacraments are called for. We must also be willing to suffer for You and for all our fellow humans, and we must die to self daily.

10.   Actually, the Church teaches us that perseverance until the end cannot be earned even by those in the state of grace. It can only be obtained through prayer. *(For more on final perseverance see The Catholic Catechism, p. 204.)*

11.   Therefore, Lord, grant us never to depart from You, for You alone are, with the Father and the Holy Spirit, the Source of all goodness, happiness and peace, as well as the Author of eternal life in Your Kingdom. Grant us the grace of constancy that we may persevere in confidence and seed-charity until the day we must appear before Your heavenly throne to learn of our eternal destiny.

12.   Jesus, thank You for the great comfort we receive in this regard when we say to Your Blessed Mother, "Pray for us sinners, now and at the hour of our death." Amen.

Try to read these Scripture passages and meditations several times a day in a reflective manner. Each time you do so, the Holy Spirit will give you more insights.
Please refer to the page immediately preceding Chapter XX, Paragraphs 1-2; Chapter XXI, Paragraphs 1-5; and Chapter XXII, Paragraphs 1-5 of our "Peaceful Seed Living" prayer and meditation book, Volume II.

Parable of the ten bridesmaids

1 **25** "Then the kingdom of heaven will be like this: Ten bridesmaids took their lamps and went to meet the bridegroom.
2 Five of them were foolish and five were sen- (C2)(C3)
3 sible: •the foolish ones did take their lamps, (C2)
4 but they brought no oil, •whereas the sensible (C3) ones took flasks of oil as well as their lamps.
5 The bridegroom was late, and they all grew
6 drowsy and fell asleep. •But at midnight there was a cry, 'The bridegroom is here! Go out
7 and meet him.' •At this, all those bridesmaids (C3)
8 woke up and trimmed their lamps, •and the foolish ones said to the sensible ones, 'Give us some of your oil: our lamps are going out.' (C2)
9 But they replied, 'There may not be enough (C3) for us and for you; you had better go to those who sell it and buy some for yourselves.'
10 They had gone off to buy it when the bridegroom arrived. Those who were ready went (C3) in with him to the wedding hall and the door (C4)
11 was closed. •The other bridesmaids arrived later. 'Lord, Lord,' they said, 'open the door (C1)
12 for us.' •But he replied, 'I tell you solemnly, (C2)
13 I do not know you.' •So stay awake, because (C4) you do not know either the day or the hour.

Parable of the talents

14 "It is like a man on his way abroad who summoned his servants and entrusted his
15 property to them. •To one he gave five talents, to another two, to a third one; each in proportion to his ability. Then he set out.
16 The man who had received the five talents promptly went and traded with them and (C3)
17 made five more. •The man who had received

18 two made two more in the same way. •But (C3) the man who had received one went off and dug a hole in the ground and hid his master's (C2) 19 money. •Now a long time after, the master of those servants came back and went 20 through his accounts with them. •The man who had received the five talents came forward bringing five more. 'Sir,' he said 'you entrusted me with five talents; here are five (C3) 21 more that I have made.' •His master said to him, 'Well done, good and faithful servant; (C3) you have shown you can be faithful in small things, I will trust you with greater; come and 22 join in your master's happiness.' •Next the man with the two talents came forward. 'Sir,' he said, 'you entrusted me with two talents; 23 here are two more that I have made.' •His (C3) master said to him, 'Well done, good and (C3) faithful servant; you have shown you can be faithful in small things, I will trust you with greater; come and join in your master's happi- 24 ness.' •Last came forward the man who had the one talent. 'Sir,' said he, 'I had heard you were a hard man, reaping where you have not sown and gathering where you have not scat- 25 tered; •so I was afraid, and I went off and hid (C2) your talent in the ground. Here it is; it was 26 yours, you have it back.' •But his master an- swered him, 'You wicked and lazy servant! (C2) So you knew that I reap where I have not sown and gather where I have not scattered? 27 Well then, you should have deposited my money with the bankers, and on my return I would have recovered my capital with inter- 28 est. •So now, take the talent from him and give it to the man who has the ten talents. 29 For to everyone who has will be given more, (C3) and he will have more than enough; but from the man who has not, even what he has will (C2) 30 be taken away. •As for this good-for-nothing (C2) servant, throw him out into the dark, where there will be weeping and grinding of teeth.'

The Last Judgment

31 "When the Son of Man comes in his glory,
escorted by all the angels, then he will take
32 his seat on his throne of glory. •All the nations will be assembled before him and he (C3)
will separate men one from another as the (C2)
33 shepherd separates sheep from goats. •He
will place the sheep on his right hand and the (C3)
34 goats on his left. •Then the King will say to (C4)
those on his right hand, 'Come, you whom (C2)
my Father has blessed, take for your heritage
the kingdom prepared for you since the foun-
35 dation of the world. •For I was hungry and (C3)
you gave me food; I was thirsty and you gave (C3)
me drink; I was a stranger and you made me (C)
36 welcome; •naked and you clothed me, sick (C3)
and you visited me, in prison and you came
37 to see me.' •Then the virtuous will say to him (C3)
in reply, 'Lord, when did we see you hungry
and feed you; or thirsty and give you drink?
38 When did we see you a stranger and make
39 you welcome; naked and clothe you; •sick or
40 in prison and go to see you?' •And the King

will answer, 'I tell you solemnly, in so far as (C3)
you did this to one of the least of these broth-
41 ers of mine, you did it to me.' •Next he will (C3)
say to those on his left hand, 'Go away from (C2)
me, with your curse upon you, to the eternal
fire prepared for the devil and his angels. (C2)
42 For I was hungry and you never gave me (C2)
food; I was thirsty and you never gave me (C2)
43 anything to drink; •I was a stranger and you (C2)
never made me welcome, naked and you (C2)
never clothed me, sick and in prison and you (C2)
44 never visited me.' •Then it will be their turn (C2)
to ask, 'Lord, when did we see you hungry
or thirsty, a stranger or naked, sick or in
45 prison, and did not come to your help?' •Then
he will answer, 'I tell you solemnly, in so far
as you neglected to do this to one of the least (C2)
46 of these, you neglected to do it to me.' •And (C2)
they will go away to eternal punishment, and
the virtuous to eternal life.'' (C3)
(C4)

Week 3 Day 4
Four C's Meditations
on St. Matthew 25:1-46

1. Jesus, Our Divine Savior, today You spoke to us again about Your role as Judge and about the perseverance Your followers must exercise if eternal salvation is to be secured. The fact You repeat these themes demonstrates that You expect us to reflect on them frequently.

2. Before dealing with the Last Judgment itself, You touched upon the need of being prepared for Your appearance as our Judge, whether at the moment of our death, or at the time of Your Second Coming to judge the world.

3. Lord, in the Parable of the Ten Bridesmaids, found in today's reading, the five sensible bridesmaids represent those who will be prepared for Your return and the five foolish ones are those who will not be ready.(121) The example of the foolish bridesmaids warns us that once You make Your appearance, it will be too late to repent in order to gain access to Your heavenly Kingdom. Consequently, our eternal destiny will be determined by whether or not we are ready to receive You at the *unexpected* moment of Your return.

4. We are also reminded of Your Parable of the Sower, in which You implied a person can be ready for Your appearance as Judge for a considerable period of time, yet fall away at

the end.*(122)* Our preparedness, then, to receive You and Your Kingdom at the moment You appear is of crucial importance.

5.   Mary, Our Queen and Mother, pray for us sinners, now and at the hour of our death.

6.   Jesus, in today's meditation, we also read the Parable of the Talents which teaches us a valuable lesson about the rewards given to those who will be ready at Your Coming. And we learned as well about the penalty for those who will not be ready.*(123)*

7.   In the mysterious designs of Your providence, You give each one of Your followers certain natural and supernatural gifts. Some have more, some have less. But to the degree the possessors use them, they will be rewarded at Your return; assuming of course, they have not fallen away in the meantime. And those who have many gifts will be expected to use them, and to use them well. As You have said elsewhere, "When a man has had a great deal given him, a great deal

will be demanded of him." *(124)* Those, on the other hand, who do not make use of their talents will be excluded from Your eternal presence.

8.   Jesus, Our Savior, King and Judge, through Your Holy Spirit, inspire us to make the best possible use of the many gifts You have given us; not only our gifts of supernatural grace, but of nature as well. May we develop greater faith and hope in You and sow ever-increasing amounts of sacrificial love for You and for others, especially for the poor and needy. And may we frequently remember that You will reward the faithful stewardship of Your gifts with inner peace, joy and happiness.

9.   In Your description of the Last Judgment, Jesus, we dwelt on the connection You made between our eternal destiny and our acts of charity. *(125)* In the last analysis, it is our consistent acts of supernatural seed-charity that will guarantee our salvation. Clearly, the many talents You have given us are to be used in charity, not only towards You but towards our fellow man as well. Thus, by sowing seeds of charity for others, we are also demonstrating our love for You. St. John said it well:

10.   "Anyone who says, 'I love God' and hates his brother is a liar, because a man who does not love his brother that he can see cannot love God, whom he has never seen. So this is the commandment he has given us,

that anyone who loves God must love his brother also."(126)

11. Help us, dear Jesus, ever to keep in mind how You will judge us on the Last Day. You will say to those on Your right hand: " 'Come, you whom my Father has blessed, take for your heritage the kingdom prepared for you . . . for I was hungry and you gave me food; I was thirsty and you gave me drink; I was a stranger and you made me welcome; naked and you clothed me, sick and you visited me, in prison and you came to see me.' "(127)

12. In Your parable about Lazarus and the rich man, we also get a glimpse of how those who are either materially or spiritually rich, or both, are to treat those who are either spiritually or materially poor, or both.(128) The message is clear: we who are rich must help those who are poor.

13. Lord, we are our brother's keeper and there are so many who need our spiritual and material help. We who are Your followers have been greatly blessed, if not materially, then certainly spiritually. Inspire us to use our wealth to help the poor and needy, many of whom may be members of our own families, and our neighbors, co-workers, and fellow parishioners. "The harvest is rich, but the laborers are few."(129) Amen.

Try to experience God's gift of peace, through the action of the Holy Spirit, by slowly re-reading and meditating on the Scripture for today.

Please refer to Chapter XXIII, Paragraphs 1 to 4 and Chapter XXIV, Paragraphs 1 to 4 of our "Peaceful Seed Living" prayer and meditation book, Volume II.

VII. PASSION AND RESURRECTION

The conspiracy against Jesus

1 **26** Jesus had now finished all he wanted
2 to say, and he told his disciples, ·"It
will be Passover, as you know, in two days'
time, and the Son of Man will be handed over
to be crucified." (C2)

3 Then the chief priests and the elders of the
people assembled in the palace of the high
4 priest, whose name was Caiaphas, ·and made
plans to arrest Jesus by some trick and (C2)
5 have him put to death. ·They said, however,
"It must not be during the festivities; there
must be no disturbance among the people."

The anointing at Bethany

6 Jesus was at Bethany in the house of Si-
7 mon the leper, when ·a woman came to him
with an alabaster jar of the most expensive
ointment, and poured it on his head as he was (C3)
8 at table. ·When they saw this, the disciples
were indignant; "Why this waste?" they said. (C2)
9 "This could have been sold at a high price
10 and the money given to the poor." ·Jesus
noticed this. "Why are you upsetting the
woman?" he said to them. "What she has
done for me is one of the good works*a* in- (C3)
11 deed! ·You have the poor with you always,
12 but you will not always have me. ·When she
poured this ointment on my body, she did it
13 to prepare me for burial. ·I tell you solemnly, (C3)

215

wherever in all the world this Good News is
proclaimed, what she has done will be told (C3)
also, in remembrance of her.''

Judas betrays Jesus

14   Then one of the Twelve, the man called
15 Judas Iscariot, went to the chief priests ·and
    said, "What are you prepared to give me if (C2)
16 I hand him over to you?" ·They paid him
    thirty silver pieces,[b] and from that moment
    he looked for an opportunity to betray him. (C2)

Preparations for the Passover supper

17   Now on the first day of Unleavened Bread[c]
    the disciples came to Jesus to say, "Where
    do you want us to make the preparations for
18 you to eat the passover?" ·"Go to so-and-
    so in the city," he replied, "and say to him,
    'The Master says: My time is near. It is at
    your house that I am keeping Passover
19 with my disciples.'" ·The disciples did
    what Jesus told them and prepared the Pass- (C3)
    over.

The treachery of Judas foretold

20   When evening came he was at table with

21 the twelve disciples. •And while they were eating he said, "I tell you solemnly, one of
22 you is about to betray me." •They were (C2) greatly distressed and started asking him in
23 turn, "Not I, Lord, surely?" •He answered, "Someone who has dipped his hand into the
24 dish with me will betray me. •The Son of Man (C2) is going to his fate, as the scriptures say he will, but alas for that man by whom the Son of Man is betrayed! Better for that man if (C2)
25 he had never been born!" •Judas, who was to betray him, asked in his turn, "Not I, (C2) Rabbi, surely?" "They are your own words," answered Jesus.

The institution of the Eucharist

26 Now as they were eating,^{d} Jesus took some bread, and when he had said the blessing he broke it and gave it to the disciples. "Take
27 it and eat;" he said, "this is my body." •Then he took a cup, and when he had returned thanks he gave it to them. "Drink all of you
28 from this," he said, •"for this is my blood, the blood of the covenant, which is to be poured out for many for the forgiveness of sins. (C3)
29 From now on, I tell you, I shall not drink wine until the day I drink the new wine with you in the kingdom of my Father."

30 After psalms had been sung^e they left for
31 the Mount of Olives. ·Then Jesus said to
them, "You will all lose faith in me this (C2)
night,^f for the scripture says: *I shall strike the* (Ci)
shepherd and the sheep of the flock will be
32 *scattered,^g* ·but after my resurrection I shall
33 go before you to Galilee." ·At this, Peter
said, "Though all lose faith in you, I will (C2)
34 never lose faith." ·Jesus answered him, "I tell (C1)
you solemnly, this very night, before the cock
crows, you will have disowned me three
35 times." ·Peter said to him, "Even if I have (C2)
to die with you, I will never disown you." (C4)
And all the disciples said the same. (C3)

Gethsemane

36 Then Jesus came with them to a small es-
tate called Gethsemane; and he said to his
disciples, "Stay here while I go over there to
37 pray." ·He took Peter and the two sons of (C3)
Zebedee with him. And sadness came over
38 him, and great distress. ·Then he said to
them, "My soul is sorrowful to the point of
death. Wait here and keep awake with me."
39 And going on a little further he fell on his
face and prayed. "My Father," he said "if it
is possible, let this cup pass me by. Nevertheless, let it be as you, not I, would have it." (C3)
40 He came back to the disciples and found
them sleeping, and he said to Peter, "So you (C2)
had not the strength to keep awake with me
41 one hour? ·You should be awake, and praying (C3)
not to be put to the test. The spirit is willing, (C4)
42 but the flesh is weak." ·Again, a second time,
he went away and prayed: "My Father," he (C3)
said, "if this cup cannot pass by without my
43 drinking it, your will be done!" ·And he came
back again and found them sleeping, their
44 eyes were so heavy. ·Leaving them there, he
went away again and prayed for the third (C3)

45 time, repeating the same words. ·Then he came back to the disciples and said to them, "You can sleep on now and take your rest. Now the hour has come when the Son of Man is to be betrayed into the hands of sin- (C2)
46 ners. ·Get up! Let us go! My betrayer is al- (C2) ready close at hand."

The arrest

47 He was still speaking when Judas, one of the Twelve, appeared, and with him a large number of men armed with swords and clubs, (C2) sent by the chief priests and elders of the
48 people. ·Now the traitor had arranged a sign (C2) with them. "The one I kiss," he had said, "he
49 is the man. Take him in charge." ·So he went straight up to Jesus and said, "Greetings,
50 Rabbi," and kissed him. ·Jesus said to him, (C2) "My friend, do what you are here for." Then they came forward, seized Jesus and took (C2)
51 him in charge. ·At that, one of the followers of Jesus grasped his sword and drew it; he struck out at the high priest's servant, and cut
52 off his ear. ·Jesus then said, "Put your sword back, for all who draw the sword will die by
53 the sword. ·Or do you think that I cannot appeal to my Father who would promptly send more than twelve legions of angels to
54 my defense? ·But then, how would the scrip- tures be fulfilled that say this is the way it
55 must be?" ·It was at this time that Jesus said to the crowds, "Am I a brigand, that you had to set out to capture me with swords and clubs? I sat teaching in the Temple day after
56 day and you never laid hands on me." ·Now all this happened to fulfill the prophecies in scripture. Then all the disciples deserted him (C2) and ran away.

Jesus before the Sanhedrin

57 The men who had arrested Jesus led him (C2) off to Caiaphas the high priest, where the scribes and the elders were assembled.

58 Peter followed him at a distance, and when he reached the high priest's palace, he went in and sat down with the attendants to see what the end would be.

59 The chief priests and the whole Sanhedrin were looking for evidence against Jesus, however false, on which they might pass the (C2)
60 death-sentence. ·But they could not find any, though several lying witnesses came forward. (C2)
61 Eventually two stepped forward ·and made a statement, "This man said, 'I have power to destroy the Temple of God and in three
62 days build it up.' " ·The high priest then stood up and said to him, "Have you no answer to that? What is this evidence these men
63 are bringing against you?" ·But Jesus was silent. And the high priest said to him, "I put you on oath by the living God to tell us if you
64 are the Christ, the Son of God." ·"The words are your own" answered Jesus. "Moreover, I tell you that from this time onward you will see the *Son of Man seated at the right hand of the Power* and *coming on the clouds of*
65 *heaven.*" ·At this, the high priest tore his clothes and said, "He has blasphemed. What (C2) need of witnesses have we now? There! You
66 have just heard the blasphemy. ·What is your (C2)

opinion?" They answered, "He deserves to die."

67 Then they spat in his face and hit him with (C2)
their fists; others said as they struck him, (C2)
68 "Play the prophet, Christ! Who hit you then?"

Peter's denials

69 Meanwhile Peter was sitting outside in the courtyard, and a servant-girl came up to him and said, "You too were with Jesus the Gali-
70 lean." •But he denied it in front of them all. (C2)
"I do not know what you are talking about," (C2)
71 he said. •When he went out to the gateway another servant-girl saw him and said to the people there, "This man was with Jesus the
72 Nazarene." •And again, with an oath, he de-
73 nied it, "I do not know the man." •A little (C2)
later the bystanders came up and said to Peter, "You are one of them for sure! Why,
74 you accent gives you away." •Then he started calling down curses on himself and swearing, (C2)

"I do not know the man." At that moment (C2)
75 the cock crew, •and Peter remembered what Jesus had said, "Before the cock crows you will have disowned me three times." And he (C3)
went outside and wept bitterly.

Week 3 Day 5
Four C's Meditations
on St. Matthew 26:1-75

1. Today, Blessed Lord, we began to read the account of Your unforgettable Passion which caused the gates of eternal glory to open to us for the first time since the Fall of our first parents. *(For an informative discussion on*

221

the origin and nature of man, including his fall from grace, read pp. 91-102 of "The Catholic Catechism.")

2.   Although You created us humans as rational creatures, we no longer act in a consistently rational manner due to the entrance of sin into our lives at the time of the Fall. This truth is quite apparent when we think of the appalling cruelty You received during the last hours of Your life on earth from those whom You loved and came to save. That You, Who are, and always were, perfectly sinless should have been treated so cruelly makes not the slightest bit of sense. The evil acts committed against You were not the result of right reason, but rather of envy, moral weakness, spiritual blindness, and hardness of heart.

3. Lord, if we were among Your first disciples, or among the Jewish or Roman authorities at the time of Your Passion, would we have treated You any better? Could we honestly say we would have been better than

Peter, who shortly before he denied You, maintained he would never do so?(130) Or would we have been less greedy than Judas, who also denied You to obtain a certain measure of wealth?(131)

4. Actually, Lord, every time we deliberately sin, we deny and betray You. Forgive us and help us to avoid doing so in the future. Help us to develop a willingness to suffer for righteousness' sake, and a willingness to die to self, rather than betray You through sin. Thus, we will become increasingly happy and holy. And we will become more capable of helping others achieve sanctity.

5. What generosity Martha's sister, Mary, showed You, Jesus, when she took the precious ointment and anointed You.(132) Its cost represented a whole year's wages for a laborer of Your day. How many of us would sacrifice a year's wages for the extension of Your Mystical Body, (the Church) on earth? Jesus, help us to be more generous with the many talents, natural and supernatural, which You have given us, remembering that to the degree that we use them in the spirit of self-sacrifice, You will more than correspondingly reward us. *("The amount you measure out is the amount you will be given — and more besides." Mark 4:24)*

6. Lord, the espisode of the precious ointment makes us realize money can and should be given to promote spiritual as well as material works. Certainly the materially poor should be helped, and their need is very great

indeed. On the other hand, there are literally hundreds of millions of people who are spiritually impoverished because they have never heard of Your liberating Gospel. Our hard-earned money, then, can be given to help them learn of You, thus enriching their hearts.

7. Most Sacred Heart of Jesus, in the account of Your institution of the Eucharist, we read words which raised our spirits. *(133)* At that very first celebration, You told Your Apostles that the bread You offered had become Your Body, and the wine, You said, was no longer wine but Your Most Precious Blood which would be poured out for the forgiveness of sins and for our salvation. You also said elsewhere that, "Anyone who does eat my flesh and drink my blood has eternal life." *(134) (For information on the Church's teaching of Christ's Body and Blood in the Eucharist, see pp. 458-465 of "The Catholic Catechism.")*

8. How fortunate we are, Lord, to be given

this sacrament. When we receive Your Real Presence under the forms of bread and wine, we are receiving, under either form, Your divine and human natures. We also participate in Your eternal sacrifice on the Cross, whereby we are strengthened to serve You, the Father and the Holy Spirit with confidence (faith and hope) and seed-charity.

9. Lord, by Your Holy Spirit, inspire us always to prepare ourselves properly for Mass, so we may enter into Your eternal sacrifice and be made acceptable to You and to the Father and to the Holy Spirit. Unite our daily sacrifices with Your eternal sacrifice to the Father.

10. Jesus, Savior, in the Garden of Gethesamane You taught us the importance of turning to God in fervent prayer when we are faced with difficult situations. You also showed us how we are to pray. Thus, while You instinctively dreaded the agony that awaited You, Your will remained firm. You freely surrendered Yourself to the Father, uttering the words which should accompany all of our petitions, "Nevertheless, let it be as You, not I would have it."(135)

11. In the account of Gethsemane, we also discovered the conduct of Peter, James and John, whom You ordered to stay awake. But instead of obeying You, Lord, drowsiness overcame them and they fell asleep. Then, You told Peter, once more, to remain awake, and to pray not to give in to temptation, but again he and the other two fell asleep.(136)

Jesus, just as You asked Your disciples in the Garden to pray for an hour, so today the Apostolate asks us to pray for up to an hour every day. Help us to accomplish this and not fall into the sleep of spiritual neglect. May we not only strive to give You an hour a day, but also to consciously live in Your presence throughout the day as we fulfill our daily tasks.

12. Lord, You warned us that every day we will have crosses to endure, such as temptations, if we are to remain loyal to You. *(137)* Each one of these calls for prayer, so we will not fall under their weight and fail to do Your will. Therefore, send us Your Holy Spirit to inspire us to pray fervently, and carry our crosses without wavering, thus finding peace of heart, and constant access to Your Most Sacred Heart.

13. Lord, today, we once more reflected on Judas' preference for ill-gained material wealth rather than for Your friendship. *(138)*

We were reminded of the Parable of the Sower, in which You taught that some people lose the gift of salvation by allowing themselves to be spiritually smothered by the allurement of riches. *(139)*

14. Jesus, may we always see material wealth in its proper place. It should never be regarded as an end in itself, nor should we place its attainment above serving You. Rather, we should first set our hearts on the Kingdom of Heaven, and on God's righteousness, and then everything we really need will be given to us. *(140)*

15. Finally, Lord, we meditated on the Jewish leaders and their use of false testimony to betray You and Your mission. *(141)* They may have been the first to have done this, but there have been many others since then. In our own time, for example, there are those who maintain, among other things, that You were only a man, that You were never raised bodily from the dead, that You never claimed to be divine, and that You even sinned. These assertions, of course, are not true, but they have misled many from accepting You as You really are, and from accepting the Church You founded for our salvation.

16. Jesus, help us and others to reject all false teaching. If we ever wonder what we must believe for our salvation, we can set our minds at rest by conforming to the doctrine of the Holy Roman Pontiff, the Successor of St. Peter, to whom You said, "I have prayed for

you that your faith may not fail." *(142)* Lord, grant that we may constantly accept that doctrine. Amen.

Try to re-read and meditate on these Scripture passages and reflections at least one more time today.

Now refer to Chapter XXV, Paragraphs 1 to 7; Chapter XXVI, Paragraphs 1-14 of our "Peaceful Seed Living" prayer and meditation book, Volume II.

Jesus is taken before Pilate

1 **27** When morning came, all the chief priests and the elders of the people met in council to bring about the death of Jesus. (C2)
2 They had him bound, and led him away to (C2) hand him over to Pilate,*a* the governor.

The death of Judas

3 When he found that Jesus had been condemned, Judas his betrayer was filled with (C2) remorse and took the thirty silver pieces back
4 to the chief priests and elders. •"I have sinned;" he said "I have betrayed innocent (C2) blood." "What is that to us?" they replied. (C2)
5 "That is your concern." •And flinging down the silver pieces in the sanctuary he made off,
6 and went and hanged himself. •The chief (C2) priests picked up the silver pieces and said, "It is against the Law to put this into the
7 treasury; it is blood-money." •So they discussed the matter and bought the potter's field with it as a graveyard for foreigners,
8 and this is why the field is called the Field
9 of Blood today. •The words of the prophet Jeremiah*b* were then fulfilled: *And they took the thirty silver pieces, the sum at which the precious One was priced by the children of*
10 *Israel,* •*and they gave them for the potter's field, just as the Lord directed me.*

Jesus before Pilate

11 Jesus, then, was brought before the governor, and the governor put to him this question, "Are you the king of the Jews?" Jesus

229

12 replied, "It is you who say it." ·But when he was accused by the chief priests and the eld-
13 ers he refused to answer at all. ·Pilate then said to him, "Do you not hear how many
14 charges they have brought against you?" ·But (C2) to the governor's complete amazement, he offered no reply to any of the charges.
15 At festival time it was the governor's practice to release a prisoner for the people, any-
16 one they chose. ·Now there was at that time a notorious prisoner whose name was Barab- (C2)
17 bas. ·So when the crowd gathered, Pilate said to them, "Which do you want me to release for you: Barabbas, or Jesus who is called
18 Christ?" ·For Pilate knew it was out of jeal- (C2) ousy that they had handed him over.
19 Now as he was seated in the chair of judgment, his wife sent him a message, "Have nothing to do with that man; I have been upset all day by a dream I had about him."

20 The chief priests and the elders, however, had persuaded the crowd to demand the release of Barabbas and the execution of Jesus. (C2) (C2)

21 So when the governor spoke and asked them, "Which of the two do you want me to release

22 for you?" they said, "Barabbas." •"But in that case," Pilate said to them "what am I to do with Jesus who is called Christ?" They all (C2)

23 said, "Let him be crucified!" •"Why?" he asked "What harm has he done?" But they shouted all the louder, "Let him be cruci- (C2) (C2)

24 fied!" •Then Pilate saw that he was making no impression, that in fact a riot was imminent. So he took some water, washed his hands in front of the crowd and said, "I am innocent of this man's blood. It is your con- (C2)

25 cern." •And the people, to a man, shouted back, "His blood be on us and on our chil- (C2)

26 dren!" •Then he released Barabbas for them. He ordered Jesus to be first scourged^c and then handed over to be crucified. (C2) (C2) (C2)

Jesus is crowned with thorns

27 The governor's soldiers took Jesus with them into the Praetorium and collected the

28 whole cohort round him. •Then they stripped

29 him and made him wear a scarlet cloak, •and having twisted some thorns into a crown they (C2)

put this on his head and placed a reed in his (C2)
right hand. To make fun of him they knelt to (C2)
30 him saying, "Hail, king of the Jews!" ·And (C2)
they spat on him and took the reed and struck (C2)
31 him on the head with it. ·And when they had
finished making fun of him, they took off the (C2)
cloak and dressed him in his own clothes and
led him away to crucify him.

The crucifixion

32 On their way out, they came across a man
from Cyrene, Simon by name, and enlisted
33 him to carry his cross. ·When they had (C3)
reached a place called Golgotha,^{d} that is, the
34 place of the skull, ·they gave him wine to
35 drink. ·When they had finished crucifying (C2)
him they shared out his clothing by casting
36 lots, ·and then sat down and stayed there
keeping guard over him.
37 Above his head was placed the charge
against him; it read: "This is Jesus, the King
38 of the Jews." ·At the same time two robbers (C2)
were crucified with him, one on the right and
one on the left.

The crucified Christ is mocked

39 The passers-by jeered at him; they shook (C2)
40 their heads and said, ·"So you would destroy
the Temple and·rebuild it in three days! Then
save yourself! If you are God's son, come
41 down from the cross!" ·The chief priests with
the scribes and elders mocked him in the (C2)
42 same way. ·"He saved others," they said; "he
cannot save himself. He is the king of Israel;
let him come down from the cross now, and
43 we will believe in him. ·He puts his trust in
God; now let God rescue him if he wants
him. For he did say, 'I am the son of God.' "
44 Even the robbers who were crucified with
him taunted him in the same way. (C2)

232

45   From the sixth hour there was darkness
46 over all the land until the ninth hour. *e* •And
about the ninth hour, Jesus cried out in a loud
voice, "Eli, Eli, lama sabachthani?" that is,
"My God, my God, why have you deserted
47 *me?"f* •When some of those who stood there
heard this, they said, "The man is calling on
48 Elijah," •and one of them quickly ran to get
a sponge which he dipped in vinegar*g* and,
putting it on a reed, gave it him to drink.
49 "Wait!" said the rest of them, "and see if
50 Elijah will come to save him." •But Jesus,
again crying out in a loud voice, yielded up
his spirit.

51   At that, the veil of the Temple*h* was torn
in two from top to bottom; the earth quaked;
52 the rocks were split; •the tombs opened and
the bodies of many holy men rose from the
53 dead, •and these, after his resurrection, came
out of the tombs, entered the Holy City and
54 appeared to a number of people. •Meanwhile
the centurion, together with the others guarding Jesus, had seen the earthquake and all
that was taking place, and they were terrified and said, "In   uth this was a son of   (CI)
God."

55   And many women were there, watching
from a distance, the same women who had
followed Jesus from Galilee and looked after
56 him. ·Among them were Mary of Magdala, (C3)
Mary the mother of James and Joseph, and
the mother of Zebedee's sons.

The burial

57   When it was evening, there came a rich
man of Arimathaea, called Joseph, who had
58 himself become a disciple of Jesus. ·This man
went to Pilate and asked for the body of
Jesus. Pilate thereupon ordered it to be (C3)
59 handed over. ·So Joseph took the body,
60 wrapped it in a clean shroud ·and put it in his (C3)
own new tomb which he had hewn out of the
rock. He then rolled a large stone across the
61 entrance of the tomb and went away. ·Now
Mary of Magdala and the other Mary were
there, sitting opposite the sepulchre.
                                          (C3)

The guard at the tomb

62   Next day, that is, when Preparation Day*i*
was over, the chief priests and the Pharisees
63 went in a body to Pilate ·and said to him,
"Your Excellency, we recall that this impos-
tor said, while he was still alive, 'After three
64 days I shall rise again.' ·Therefore give the
order to have the sepulchre kept secure until
the third day, for fear his disciples come and
steal him away and tell the people, 'He has
risen from the dead.' This last piece of fraud
would be worse than what went before."
65 "You may have your guard" said Pilate to
them. "Go and make all as secure as you
66 know how." ·So they went and made the sepulchre secure, putting seals on the stone and
mounting a guard.

Week 3 Day 6
Four C's Meditations
on St. Matthew 27:1-66

1.   In today's meditation, Lord, we were told of Judas' remorse in betraying You. That in itself is commendable. But we noted further that he had no faith in You, since in despair, he took his own life. The particular horror of a suicide, in which the self-killer is fully responsible, is that of an unrepented sin. All sins, if repented in this life, You mercifully forgive. We have no assurance, however, that grave sins unrepented in this life, and willfully committed, can be forgiven after death. *(It would seem from the Gospel accounts that Judas was fully responsible for taking his life. Consequently, it could be said that he was fully responsible for committing a grave or mortal sin, separating himself from God's saving grace. On the other hand, there are suicides who are not fully responsible for their acts of self-destruction. Such persons, are not, in God's eyes, guilty of committing mortal sin. Thus the possibility of eternal salvation has not been denied them because of their self-murder. Since God is the final judge of human conduct, we can be thankful it does not fall upon us to determine whether or not a suicide has been denied access to God's Kingdom.)*

2. Jesus, by the guidance of Your Holy Spirit, help each one of us to examine our consciences daily to repent of our sins sincerely so we can receive Your gracious forgiveness.

3. Next, Lord, we dwelled on the moral weakness of Pilate, the Roman governor. Although he was convinced You were innocent of the trumped-up charges against You, he refused to release You because of the strong opposition of the Jewish leaders and the crowd they had incited against You.

4. Pilate's weakness reminds us of the fact that pressure from others can, at times, tempt us almost unbearably to act against our consciences. Yet, Lord, we do not have to give in to outside pressures of this sort, since You give those in Your friendship the grace to effectively resist them.

5. When, with Your grace, we begin to say, "No," to such influences, we can be sure we are making significant progress in the spiritual life, since we are placing You and Your will first in our lives. Lord, inspire us to rise above the temptations to sin that others place before us from time to time, and may we never be sources of temptations and scandal for them. Help us to rely on Your strength, and not on our own, to avoid sin. May the memory of Peter's denial assist us in this regard.

6. Jesus, St. Matthew reveals to us how You were shamefully and cruelly treated by those whom You came to save. You were

falsely accused of criminal activity. You were betrayed by those who knew You to be innocent. You were denied by Your friends. You were jeered at by the crowd. You were whip-lashed, tortured, mocked, and finally given the criminal's execution. Yet all the while You willingly accepted this cruel agony for the sake of us unworthy sinners. What charity You possessed, Lord, and how little we appreciate it — as our constant sinning bears witness.

7. "A man can have no greater love than to lay down his life for his friends."*(143)* "It is not easy to die even for a good man — though of course for someone really worthy, men might be prepared to die — but what proves that God still loves us is that Christ had died for us while we were still sinners."*(144)* "Why, Christ Himself, innocent though He was, had died once for sins, died for the guilty, to lead us to God."*(145)*

8. You gladly suffered and died for us, Lord, because You loved us. But Yours is not a blind love which overlooks our sins and

demands nothing from us in return. Not at all! Rather, You sacrificed Yourself for us, so that with Your help, we would be able to imitate Your example of complete self-sacrifice to the Father and to His will, and share in His divine life for all eternity. Lord, help us daily to take up our crosses and follow You Who are the Way, the Truth and the Life.

9. Jesus, compassionate Savior, while many betrayed and deserted You during Your Passion, there were others who had remained loyal. Among them were Mary Magdalene, Mary, the mother of James and Joseph, and the unnamed mother of the sons of Zebedee, James and John. *(146)* And, of course, there was the Apostle John and Your Blessed Mother. It is significant, we think that these were predominantly women, the so-called weaker sex, who persevered in their loyalty to You. These also portray the truth that those who were filled with Your grace need not desert You, even under the worst of circumstances.

10. Basically, Lord, our wills play a crucial role in whether or not we remain constant in our love for You. And although Your grace is absolutely necessary for us to please You completely, it never forces us to do so. Thus, when we exercise the supernatural virtue of charity, we do so freely with Your never-failing support. Consequently, the power to please or reject You, remains to a great extent in the free exercise of our wills. May we never forget this, Jesus. And, may we often reflect on the lives of the saints who freely

persevered to the end as Your faithful and loving disciples.

11.   The life and persevering love of Your Blessed Mother deserves our special consideration, because of her unequalled sanctity. May we turn to her frequently for the comfort of her maternal protection.

12.   Remember, O most gracious Virgin Mary, that never was it known that anyone who fled to Your protection, implored Your help or sought Your intercession was left unaided. Inspired by this confidence, I fly to You, O Virgin of Virgins, my Mother. To You I come, before You I stand, sinful and sorrowful. O Mother of the Word of Incarnate, do not ignore my petitions, but in Your mercy hear and answer me. Amen.

Try to read these Scripture passages and meditations several times a day in a reflective manner. Each time you do so, the Holy Spirit will give you more insights.

Please refer to Chapter XXVII, Paragraphs 1 to 4 of our "Peaceful Seed Living" prayer and meditation book, Volume II.

The empty tomb. The angel's message

1 **28** After the sabbath, and toward dawn on the first day of the week, Mary of Magdala and the other Mary went to visit the 2 sepulchre. •And all at once there was a vio- (C3) lent earthquake, for the angel of the Lord, descending from heaven, came and rolled 3 away the stone and sat on it. •His face was 4 like lightning, his robe white as snow. •The guards were so shaken, so frightened of him, 5 that they were like dead men. •But the angel spoke; and he said to the women, "There is no need for you to be afraid. I know you are 6 looking for Jesus, who was crucified. •He is not here, for he has risen, as he said he would. Come and see the place where he lay, 7 then go quickly and tell his disciples, 'He has (C3) risen from the dead and now he is going before you to Galilee; it is there you will see 8 him.' Now I have told you." •Filled with awe and great joy the women came quickly away from the tomb and ran to tell the disciples. (C3)

Appearance to the women

9 And there, coming to meet them, was Jesus. "Greetings," he said. And the women came up to him and, falling down before him, (C3) 10 clasped his feet. •Then Jesus said to them "Do not be afraid; go and tell my brothers that they must leave for Galilee; they will see me there."

Precautions taken by the leaders of the people

11 While they were on their way, some of the guard went off into the city to tell the chief

12 priests all that had happened. •These held a
meeting with the elders and, after some discussion, handed a considerable sum of
13 money to the soldiers •with these instructions, "This is what you must say, 'His disciples came during the night and stole him ⁽ᶜ²⁾
14 away while we were asleep.' •And should the
governor come to hear of this, we undertake
to put things right with him ourselves and to
15 see that you do not get into trouble." •The
soldiers took the money and carried out their
instructions, and to this day that is the story ⁽ᶜ²⁾
among the Jews.

Appearance in Galilee. The mission to the world

16 Meanwhile the eleven disciples set out for ⁽ᶜ³⁾
Galilee, to the mountain where Jesus had ar-
17 ranged to meet them. •When they saw him ⁽ᶜ³⁾
they fell down before him, though some hesi-
18 tated. •Jesus came up and spoke to them. He
said, "All authority in heaven and on earth
19 has been given to me. •Go, therefore, make
disciples of all the nations; baptize them in ⁽ᶜ³⁾
the name of the Father and of the Son and
20 of the Holy Spirit,ᵃ •and teach them to observe all the commands I gave you. And ⁽ᶜ³⁾
know that I am with you always; yes, to the ⁽ᶜ³⁾
end of time." ⁽ᶜ⁴⁾

241

Week 3 Day 7
Four C's Meditations
on St. Matthew 28:1-20

1. Heavenly Father, for twenty-one days we have been meditating on the life and teachings of Your divine Son Who became man so we could become Your saints. During this period we have noted these things in particular: His relentless trust in You, His undefiled conscience, and His unremitting acts of seed-charity for You and for us. And yesterday, we considered His supreme act of seed-charity, the offering of Himself on the Cross as a sacrifice for our sins.

2. In today's reading, we were given St. Matthew's account of that miracle of miracles, the bodily Resurrection of Jesus from the dead. It was this miracle which served to convince His followers, beyond every shadow of doubt, that He was both God and man — and the long-expected Messiah Who conquered not only sin, but death which is the fruit of sin.

3. It seems unlikely that if there had been no Resurrection, the Apostles would have accepted Jesus as the Messiah, and would have been willing to give up everything to spread the Gospel to the ends of the earth. In all probability, if there had been no Resurrection, there would have been only the memory of His cruel death on the Cross, which would have seemed more like a defeat by the forces of evil than the saving sacrifice it was.

4.   These considerations remind us of St. Paul's words in I Corinthians 15:

5.   "If there is no resurrection of the dead, Christ himself cannot have been raised, and If Christ has not been raised then our preaching is useless and your believing it is useless; indeed, we are shown up as witnesses who have committed a perjury before God, because we swore in evidence before God that He had raised Christ to life."*(147)*

6.   These words remind us also, Father, that Your Son's glorious Resurrection from the dead is the basis for our belief that we shall also be raised bodily on the Last Day. Thus, if Jesus had not conquered death, then it would obviously be impossible for us to do so as well.

7.   Still there are false teachers, today, who either deny or question Jesus' bodily Resurrection. Most Holy Father, Your Son's Resurrection is the clear teaching of Scripture and an unchangeable dogma of the Catholic Church. May we never doubt or deny it.

8.   In today's Scripture reading, Father, we noted too the charity of Mary Magdalene and the other Mary, who very early that Sunday morning went to visit the tomb of Your dear Son.*(148)*

9.   Mary Magdalene's charity is especially striking in view of her past life. Having been a woman of ill-repute, she finally turned to Your Son in faith, trust and repentance, and received the forgiveness of her sins. She then, with Your help, became a great saint.

10. Heavenly Father, the example of St. Mary Magdalene reminds us that Your beloved Son, in His great charity, always offers us sinners His friendship and forgiveness which we can freely receive when we turn to Him with our whole heart.

11. We also observed in our meditation, Heavenly Father, that there were those who sought to frustrate Your eternal plan for our salvation by their lies, deceits and bribes. *(149)*

12. Even today, people exist who seek to turn us away from Your Son and His Holy Catholic Church. Some of these people do so with evil consciences. Others, misguided though they may be, do so with the sincere belief they are serving the truth.

13. Lord, it is a provable fact that only the Catholic Church, over the centuries, has kept pure and intact the doctrine entrusted by Your Son and the Holy Spirit to the Apostles. Constantly inspire us to share this same doctrine with those who presently reject it, in

whole or in part. Especially help us to bring to Christ those who actively seek to turn people away from the Gospel.

14.   As a matter of fact, the desire to share the Gospel with others, is not really an option for Christians. It is a duty imposed upon us by Our Lord Himself shortly before he ascended into Heaven. Addressing Himself to the Apostles, He said, "Go therefore, make disciples of all the nations. . .and teach them to observe all the commandments I gave you."*(150)*

15.   That this responsibility includes lay members of the Church is made clear by the teaching of Vatican II in its document on the lay apostolate.

16.   "And the precept of charity, which is the Lord's greatest commandment, urges all Christians to work for the glory of God through the coming of his kingdom and for the communication of eternal life to all men, that they may know the only true God and Jesus Christ whom he sent." (Austin Flannery, O.P.(ed.) "Vatican Council II," pp. 769.)

17.   Again, Vatican II taught, "In the concrete, their apostolate (i.e., the laity's) is exercised when they work at the evangelization and sanctification of men."*(Ibid. p. 768.)*

18.   Almighty Father, as we conclude our daily meditations on the life and teaching of Your eternal son, we offer You our profound thanks for giving Him to us. For it was through His infinite charity that we have been

reconciled to You. Grant that we may always follow Him and His doctrine of salvation, remembering He has promised to be with us as our Support and Mainstay until the end of time. *(151)*

19.   Pour forth, we beg You, O Lord, Your grace into our hearts: that we to whom the Incarnation of Christ Your Son was made known by the message of angel, may by His Passion and Cross be brought to the glory of His Resurrection. Through the same Christ Our Lord. Amen.

The more you re-read these Scriptures and meditations, the more you will get out of them.

Please refer to Chapter XXVIII, Paragraphs 1 to 3 and Chapter XXIX of our "Peaceful Seed Living" prayer and meditation book, Volume II.

References to Scripture

(1) Matthew 6:20
(2) 2 Corinthians 1:3-4; Galatians 4:5
(3) Matthew 5:17
(4) Deuteronomy 6:5; Leviticus 19:18
(5) Matthew 6:4
(6) Matthew 6:1
(7) Matthew 6:5-18
(8) Matthew 6:19-21;24
(9) Matthew 6:25-34
(10) Matthew 6:11
(11) Matthew 6:13
(12) I Peter 5:8; I Corinthians 10:13
(13) Matthew 6:12
(14) Matthew 7:1-5
(15) Acts 1:24;15:8
(16) Matthew 7:7
(17) Romans 11:33-34
(18) Matthew 7:12
(19) I Timothy 2:4; 2 Corinthians 5:14-15
(20) Matthew 7:13-14
(21) Matthew 7:15-20
(22) Matthew 7:21-27
(23) I Corinthians 13
(24) Matthew 7:24-27
(25) Philippians 4:7
(26) Matthew 8:1-3;5:13
(27) Matthew 8:23-27
(28) Matthew 28:20
(29) Matthew 9:18-26
(30) Matthew 9:27-31
(31) Matthew 8:5-13
(32) Matthew 9:3;34
(33) Matthew 9:32-34
(34) Matthew 9:13

(71) I Corinthians 10:13
(72) Matthew 24:13
(73) Matthew 15:1-9
(74) Matthew 15:21-28
(75) John 6:47-51; Matthew 26:26-28;18-20
(76) Matthew 25:35-46
(77) Matthew 16:5-12
(78) Matthew 16:16
(79) Matthew 6:25-34;28:20
(80) 2 Corinthians 1:3-4
(81) Matthew 16:24
(82) Matthew 17:14-20
(83) Matthew 17:20
(84) Matthew 18:1
(85) Matthew 18:3-4
(86) Matthew 18:5-10
(87) Matthew 18:12-14
(88) Matthew 18:15-17
(89) Matthew 18:21-22
(90) Matthew 19:3-9
(91) Matthew 19:13-15
(92) Matthew 19:23-26
(93) Matthew 19:16-22
(94) I Timothy 6:10
(95) Matthew 19:27-30
(96) Matthew 20:1-16
(97) Matthew 20:20-23
(98) 2 Timothy 3:12; Acts 14:22
(99) I Peter 4:14
(100) Matthew 20:25-28
(101) Matthew 25:40
(102) Matthew 21:9
(103) Matthew 21:18-22
(104) Matthew 28:28-32
(105) I Corinthians 13:1-3
(106) Matthew 21:33-46

The Work and Goals of the Apostolate

Purpose

The Apostolate for Family Consecration is an international community of believers whose specific purpose and unique role in the Church is to reinforce the Christian family through the systematic transformation of neighborhoods into God-centered communities. As a result of the establishment of enough of these "God-centered communities," a nation will advance significantly on the spiritual plane, and in most instances, even on the material level. "Virtue makes a nation great, by sin whole races are disgraced." *(Proverbs 14:34)* "Happy is the nation whose God is the Lord."*(Psalms 33:12)* "'. . . Bad friends ruin the noblest of people." *(I Cor. 15:33)*

Motto

All for the Sacred and Eucharistic Heart of Jesus, all through the Sorrowful and Immaculate Heart of Mary, all in union with St. Joseph.

Spirituality

The four biblical pillars of the Apostolate's "Peaceful Seed Living" spirituality are Confidence, Conscience, seed-Charity and Constancy. When a person builds his or her daily life on these four pillars, he or she will be living a life of true union with God and will be blessed with a peaceful heart that only God can give.

"All Scripture is inspired by God and can

profitably be used for teaching, for refuting error, for guiding people's lives and teaching them to be holy. *(2 Tim 3:16)*

Our spiritual goal is to develop a deep interior union with the Holy Spirit of God. The best way to achieve this mystical union is by increasing not the number of prayers said but the fervor and time invested in prayer and meditation every day. When we convert our daily trials encountered through the fulfillment of our responsibilities into sacrifices for God, we actually unite ourselves with Christ's sacrifice of the Mass at Calvary. Only through these spiritual means, can we restore man's relationship with God and loosen the diabolical hold the forces of evil have on so many families, schools, neighborhoods, our country and the entire world.

Act of Consecration

The Act of Total Consecration to the Holy Family which the Apostolate promotes, offers all of a person's spiritual and material possessions for the Sacred and Eucharistic Heart of Jesus, through the Sorrowful and Immaculate Heart of Mary, in union with St. Joseph.

Through this act of total consecration, individuals are asking to be purified and used as God's instruments by the Holy Family. It is recognized that the Holy Family can do far more good with people's humble possessions than they ever could on their own. We believe that this offering enables God to multiply an individual's merits and offset the effects of sin in the world. *(2 Cor. 9:10)*

People who are totally consecrated give all of their indulgences to the Holy Family to relieve the suffering of loved ones and other Poor Souls in Purgatory. The Poor Souls are asked to continually pray that all the members of our families and the members and families of the Apostolate fulfill, to the fullest extent, the Father's distinctive plan for their lives.

Our Cooperator, Chapter and Apostolic members are required to make this act of total consecration. Other members and individuals who participate in our "Neighborhood Peace of Heart Forums" are encouraged, but not required, to also totally consecrate themselves to the Holy Family.

The Church's Guide and Incentive for Holiness

The Apostolate uses the Church's norms for indulgences as a specific guide for achieving a balanced, God-centered life in the modern world, while asking its members to perform heroic acts of charity by giving their indulgences to the Poor Souls in purgatory.

Neighborhood Chapter Programs

Our goal, God willing, is to establish, within every nation, a national network of Neighborhood Chapters capable of continually educating and motivating people to place God first in their lives. These chapters will perform four distinct functions:

• Change personal attitudes of neighborhood residents through in-depth and continuous "Neighborhood Peace of Heart Forums."

• Deepen personal commitment and effectiveness through total consecration to the Holy Family through our home visitation programs.

• Consolidate neighborhoods through public devotions in our churches.

• Cultivate our youth through our youth leadership program.

When Chapters are Established

After enough Neighborhood Chapters are established in an area, the Apostolate will utilize the media as a positive means to draw people into our in-depth formation programs.

We will also establish, within the area, a combination audio-visual lending library, religious book store and gift shop operated by our members.

Types of Membership

Membership is open to all who qualify and fulfill the following conditions:

A. Sacri-State members are those who offer up as a sacrifice of their state in life, their trials encountered in the faithful fulfillment of their responsibilities. They recognize the fact these sacrifices are not only meritorious, but if specifically willed, are also indulgenced by the Church.

Sacri-State members freely entrust either part or all of their merits and indulgences, earned from their prayers and sacrifices, to be distributed by the Holy Family. The Holy Family is asked to apply the merits of the members toward the work of the Apostolate, and to apply their indulgences for their loved ones and other Poor Souls in Purgatory.

We ask the Poor Souls helped by our indulgences to continually pray that all the members of our family and the members and families of the Apostolate fulfill the Father's distinctive plan for their lives. This commitment need only be made once and may be revoked by a specific act of the will at any time. Sacri-State members do not have to totally consecrate themselves to the Holy Family.

Sacri-State membership is a spiritual bond and, therefore, no formal application is necessary. One need only submit a note indicating a willingness to fulfill these conditions. There are also no dues for Sacri-State members.

If you belong to a religious community or an organized apostolic group, your entire community can join and become a Sacri-State community of the Apostolate.

B. Cooperator members are those who fulfill the conditions for Sacri-State membership, and also totally consecrate themselves to the Holy Family, and strive to follow the recommended practices, and recite the recommended prayers of the Apostolate for Family Consecration.

In addition, to become a Cooperator member, one should send for our formal application form and submit it for certification. Cooperator members may also be candidates for the following Apostolic or Chapter memberships.

C. Chapter members are those who are totally consecrated to the Holy Family and have successfully completed our candidate program, while actively working in the Apostolate on a voluntary basis.

D. Apostolic members are those who are totally consecrated to the Holy Family and have successfully completed our candidate program, while having committed themselves to devote at least one year in the work of the Apostolate on a full time basis.

E. Benefactor members are those individuals who contribute the much needed financial assistance to the Apostolate for Family Consecration. One may be a Benefactor member and also one of the other mentioned members.

Benefits of Membership

In unity there is strength. Our living and deceased members and their families will be remembered in all of the Masses offered for the Apostolate and its work.

In addition, all living and deceased members and their families will be remembered through the perpetual vigil lights in the sanctuary of the Sacred Hearts Chapel at the House of St. Joseph.

All members of the Apostolate are actually part of a community of believers who share in the prayers and merits of the other members throughout the world. We particularly ask our members to pray on Fridays for the specific petitions sent in to the Apostolate.

St. Paul said: "The more you sow, the more you reap." *(2 Cor. 9:6)* When you pray for others, you plant a seed of love that will bear an abundant harvest for your loved ones, yourselves and the entire Mystical Body of Christ.

All members who have been properly enrolled and wear the Brown Scapular, or Scapular medal of Our Lady of Mount Carmel, qualify for the Sabbatine Privilege and share in the combined good works of the entire Carmelite Order throughout the world and over 200 million members of the Scapular Confraternity.

Those who become associated with one of our neighborhood chapters will also receive the companionship and support of individuals holding like moral and spiritual convictions. In addition, our members will receive the great satisfaction of being able to make both their spiritual and temporal efforts count through their development of truly God-centered communities, which will nourish sound moral families in their local areas.

Those members who consecrate them-selves totally to the Holy Family (to Jesus, through Mary, in union with St. Joseph) will receive an abundance of grace by becoming the Holy Family's consecrated children.

Those who donate their time and resources to the Apostolate will receive many partial indulgences for their good works.

All members of the Apostolate are spiritually united with Mother Teresa of Calcutta and all Missionaries of Charity throughout the world. On April 22, 1978, Mother Teresa, who is a member of our Advisory Council, signed up all of the members of her community as Sacri-State members of the Apostolate for Family

Consecration. Therefore, all members of the Apostolate are spiritually united with Mother Teresa's community, and many other communities and generous individuals throughout the world, who are praying and suffering for our work. Indeed, when you combine this powerhouse of prayer and sacrifice with the prayers of the many souls being released from Purgatory because of our practices, our goal to be used as an instrument of the Holy Family to transform neighborhoods into God-centered communities will certainly be accomplished.

Litany of the Sacred Heart of Jesus

L. Lord, have mercy on us.
A. Christ, have mercy on us.

L. Lord, have mercy on us.
Christ, hear us.
A. Christ, graciously hear us.

God, the Father of Heaven, *Have mercy on us.*

God the Son, Redeemer of the
world, *Have mercy on us.*

God the Holy Ghost, *Have mercy on us.*

Holy Trinity, one God, *Have mercy on us.*

Heart of Jesus, Son of the
Eternal Father, *Have mercy on us.*

Heart of Jesus, formed by the
Holy Ghost in the Virgin
Mother's womb, *Have mercy on us.*

Heart of Jesus, substantially united to the Word of God, *Have mercy on us.*

Heart of Jesus, of infinite majesty, *Have mercy on us.*

Heart of Jesus, holy temple of God, *Have mercy on us.*

Heart of Jesus, tabernacle of the Most High, *Have mercy on us.*

Heart of Jesus, house of God and gate of Heaven, *Have mercy on us.*

Heart of Jesus, glowing furnace of charity, *Have mercy on us.*

Heart of Jesus, vessel of justice and love, *Have mercy on us.*

Heart of Jesus, full of goodness and love, *Have mercy on us.*

Heart of Jesus, abyss of all virtues, *Have mercy on us.*

Heart of Jesus, most worthy of all praise, and knowledge, *Have mercy on us.*

Heart of Jesus, wherein dwells
all the fullness of the Godhead, *Have mercy on us.*

Heart of Jesus, in Whom the
Father is wed, *Have mercy on us.*

Heart of Jesus, of Whose
fullness we have all received, *Have mercy on us.*

Heart of Jesus, desire of the
everlasting hills, *Have mercy on us.*

Heart of Jesus, patient and rich
in mercy, *Have mercy on us.*

Heart of Jesus, rich unto all who
call upon Thee, *Have mercy on us.*

Heart of Jesus, fount of life and
holiness, *Have mercy on us.*

Heart of Jesus, propitiation for
our offenses, *Have mercy on us.*

Heart of Jesus, overwhelmed
with reproaches, *Have mercy on us.*

Heart of Jesus, bruised for our
iniquities, *Have mercy on us.*

Heart of Jesus, obedient even
unto death, *Have mercy on us.*

Heart of Jesus, pierced with a
lance, *Have mercy on us.*

Heart of Jesus, source of all
consolation, *Have mercy on us.*

Heart of Jesus, our life and
resurrection, *Have mercy on us.*

Heart of Jesus, our peace and
reconciliation, *Have mercy on us.*

Heart of Jesus, victim for our sins,	*Have mercy on us.*
Heart of Jesus, salvation of those who hope in Thee,	*Have mercy on us.*
Heart of Jesus, hope of those who die in Thee,	*Have mercy on us.*
Heart of Jesus, delight of all Saints,	*Have mercy on us.*
Lamb of God, Who takest away the sins of the world,	*Spare us, O Lord.*
Lamb of God, Who takest away the sins of the world,	*Graciously hear us, O Lord.*
Lamb of God, Who takest away the sins of the world.	*Have mercy on us.*
Jesus, meek and humble of Heart,	*Make our hearts like unto Thine.*

Let us pray.

Almighty and everlasting God, look upon the Heart of Thy well-beloved Son and upon the praise and satisfaction which He offers unto Thee in the name of sinners; and do Thou of Thy great goodness grant them pardon when they seek Thy mercy, in the name of Thy Son, Jesus Christ, who liveth and reigneth with Thee for ever and ever. Amen.

The Litany of Our Lady of Loreto

L. Lord, have mercy on us.
A. Christ, have mercy on us.

L. Lord, have mercy on us.
Christ, hear us.
A. Christ, graciously hear us.

God the Father of Heaven, *Have mercy on us.*

God the Son, Redeemer of the world, *Have mercy on us.*

God the Holy Ghost, *Have mercy on us.*

Holy Trinity, one God, *Have mercy on us.*

Holy Mary, *Pray for us.*

Holy Mother of God, *Pray for us.*

Holy Virgin of virgins, *Pray for us.*

Mother of Christ, *Pray for us.*

Mother of divine grace, *Pray for us.*

Mother most pure, *Pray for us.*

Mother most chaste, *Pray for us.*

Mother inviolate, *Pray for us.*

Mother undefiled, *Pray for us.*

Mother most amiable, *Pray for us.*

Mother most admirable, *Pray for us.*

Mother of good counsel, *Pray for us.*

Mother of our Creator, *Pray for us.*

Mother of our Savior,	*Pray for us.*
Virgin most prudent,	*Pray for us.*
Virgin most venerable,	*Pray for us.*
Virgin most renowned,	*Pray for us.*
Virgin most powerful,	*Pray for us.*
Virgin most merciful,	*Pray for us.*
Virgin most faithful,	*Pray for us.*
Mirror of justice,	*Pray for us.*
Seat of wisdom,	*Pray for us.*
Cause of joy,	*Pray for us.*
Spiritual vessel,	*Pray for us.*
Vessel of honor,	*Pray for us.*
Singular vessel of devotion,	*Pray for us.*
Mystical rose,	*Pray for us.*
Tower of David,	*Pray for us.*
Tower of ivory,	*Pray for us.*
House of gold,	*Pray for us.*
Ark of the covenant,	*Pray for us.*
Gate of Heaven,	*Pray for us.*
Morning star,	*Pray for us.*
Health of the sick,	*Pray for us.*
Refuge of sinners,	*Pray for us.*

Comforter of the afflicted,	*Pray for us.*
Help of Christians,	*Pray for us.*
Queen of Angels,	*Pray for us.*
Queen of Patriarchs,	*Pray for us.*
Queen of Prophets,	*Pray for us.*
Queen of Apostles,	*Pray for us.*
Queen of Martyrs,	*Pray for us.*
Queen of Confessors,	*Pray for us.*
Queen of Virgins,	*Pray for us.*
Queen of all Saints,	*Pray for us.*
Queen conceived without original sin,	*Pray for us.*
Queen of the most holy Rosary,	*Pray for us.*
Queen of peace,	*Pray for us.*

Lamb of God, Who takest away
the sins of the world,   *Spare us, O Lord.*

Lamb of God, Who takest away
the sins of the world,   *Graciously hear us,*
                                          O Lord.

Lamb of God, Who takest away
the sins of the world,   *Have mercy on us.*

Pray for us, O holy Mother of
God,   *That we may be*
                                          made worthy of the
                                          promises of Christ.

Let us pray.

Grant, we beseech Thee, O Lord God, unto us Thy servants, that we may rejoice in continual health of mind and body; and, by the glorious intercession of blessed Mary ever Virgin, may be delivered from present sadness, and enter into the joy of Thine eternal gladness. Through Christ our Lord. Amen.

Litany of St. Joseph

Leader - Lord, have mercy on us.
All - Christ, have mercy on us.

Lord, have mercy on us;
Christ hear us,

*Christ, graciously
hear us.*

God, the Father of heaven,

Have mercy on us.

God, the Son, Redeemer of the
world,

Have mercy on us.

God, the Holy Spirit,

Have mercy on us.

Holy Trinity, One God,

Have mercy on us.

Holy Mary,

Pray for us.

St. Joseph,

*Pray for us (or)
thank you.*

Renowned offspring of David,

*Pray for us (or)
thank you.*

Splendor of Patriarchs,

*Pray for us (or)
thank you.*

Spouse of the Mother of God,

*Pray for us (or)
thank you.*

Chaste guardian of the Virgin,

*Pray for us (or)
thank you.*

Foster father of the Son of God,

*Pray for us (or)
thank you.*

Watchful defender of Christ,

*Pray for us (or)
thank you.*

Head of the Holy Family,	*Pray for us (or) thank you.*
Joseph most just,	*Pray for us (or) thank you.*
Joseph most pure,	*Pray for us (or) thank you.*
Joseph most prudent,	*Pray for us (or) thank you.*
Joseph most courageous,	*Pray for us (or) thank you.*
Joseph most obedient,	*Pray for us (or) thank you.*
Joseph most faithful,	*Pray for us (or) thank you.*
Mirror of patience,	*Pray for us (or) thank you.*
Lover of poverty,	*Pray for us (or) thank you.*
Model for all who work,	*Pray for us (or) thank you.*
Glory of family life,	*Pray for us (or) thank you.*

Guardian of virgins,	*Pray for us (or) thank you.*
Mainstay of families,	*Pray for us (or) thank you.*
Comfort of the afflicted,	*Pray for us (or) thank you.*
Hope of the sick,	*Pray for us (or) thank you.*
Patron of the dying,	*Pray for us (or) thank you.*
Terror of the demons,	*Pray for us (or) thank you.*
Protector of the Holy Church,	*Pray for us (or) thank you.*
Lamb of God, Who takest away the sins of the world,	*Spare us, O Lord.*
Lamb of God, Who takest away the sins of the world,	*Graciously hear us, O Lord.*
Lamb of God, Who takest away the sins of the world,	*Have mercy on us.*
He made him lord over His household.	*And ruler of all His possessions.*

Let us pray

My God, Who in Your unspeakable providence did grant to choose blessed Joseph to be the spouse of Your own most holy Mother, grant we beg You, that we may have him for our mediator in heaven, whom we venerate as our defender on earth, who lives and reigns world without end. Amen.

Chaplet of the Divine Mercy

In the early 1930's, Sister M. Faustina, of the Congregation of the Sisters of Our Lady of Mercy, was visited by Our Lord and entrusted with a wonderful message of Mercy for all mankind.

"Tell distressed mankind to nestle close to My merciful Heart, and I will fill them with peace...Mankind will not find peace until it turns with confidence to My Mercy."

Jesus taught her to say this prayer on ordinary rosary beads:

"First say one **'Our Father', 'Hail Mary'** *and* **'I believe'.**

Then on the large beads say the following words:

'Eternal Father, I offer You the Body and Blood, Soul and Divinity of Your dearly beloved Son, Our Lord Jesus Christ, in atonement for our sins and those of the whole world.'

On the smaller beads you are to say the following words:

'For the sake of His sorrowful Passion have mercy on us and on the whole world.'

After the five decades you are to say these words three times:

'Holy God, Holy Mighty One, Holy Immortal One, have mercy on us and on the whole world.'"

Jesus said later to Sister Faustina: "I want the whole world to know My infinite Mercy. I want to give unimaginable graces to those who trust in My Mercy."

Primarily responsible for the resurgence of the devotion to the Divine Mercy was the Archbishop of Sister Faustina's home diocese of Cracow, Poland, Karol Cardinal Wojtyla, now Pope John Paul II.

Jesus, I Trust in You!

HYMNS TAKEN FROM THE AFC FAMILY HYMNAL

The hymn numbers correspond with the complete AFC Family Hymnals and sing-a-long tapes.

1. IMMACULATE MARY

Immaculate Mary, your praises we sing.
You reign now in splendor with Jesus our King.
Ave, Ave, Ave Maria! Ave, Ave Maria!

In heaven the blessed your glory proclaim,
On earth we your children invoke your sweet name.
Ave, Ave, Ave Maria! Ave, Ave Maria!

We pray for the Church, our true Mother on earth,
And beg you to watch o'er the land of our birth.
Ave, Ave, Ave Maria! Ave, Ave Maria!

3. WERE YOU THERE

Were you there when they crucified my Lord?
Were you there when they crucified my Lord? Oh
Sometimes it causes me to tremble, tremble, tremble.
Were you there when they crucified my Lord?

Were you there when they nailed him
    to the tree?
Were you there when they nailed him
    to the tree? Oh
Sometimes it causes me to tremble,
    tremble, tremble.
Were you there when they nailed him
    to the tree?

Were you there when they laid him in
    the tomb?
Were you there when they laid him in
    the tomb? Oh
Sometimes it causes me to tremble,
    tremble, tremble.
Were you there when they laid him in
    the tomb?

9. COME, HOLY GHOST, CREATOR BLEST

Come, Holy Ghost, Creator blest,
And in our hearts take up thy rest
Come with thy grace and heav'nly aid
To fill the hearts which thou hast
    made.
To fill the hearts which thou hast
    made.

O Comforter, to thee we cry,
Thou gift of God sent from on high,
Thou font of life and fire of love,
The soul's anointing from above.
The soul's anointing from above.

Make thou to us the Father known,
Through thee his Son in faith be
  shown;
Be this our never changing creed:
That thou dost from them both
  proceed.
That thou dost from them both
  proceed.

To God the Father let us sing,
To God the Son our risen King,
And equally let us adore
The Spirit, God for evermore.
The Spirit, God for evermore.

11. HAIL, HOLY QUEEN

Hail, holy Queen enthroned above,
  Salve Regina!
Hail, Queen of mercy, Queen of love,
  Salve Regina!
Sing her praise, ye Cherubim! Join our
  song, ye Seraphim!
Heav'n and earth resound the hymn:
  Salve, Salve, Salve Regina!

Our life, our sweetness here below,
  Salve Regina!
From you all grace and comfort flow,
  Salve Regina!
Sing her praise, ye Cherubim! Join our
  song, ye Seraphim!
Heav'n and earth resound the hymn:
  Salve, Salve, Salve Regina!

Our advocate with God on high, Salve
Regina!
To you our pleading voices cry, Salve
Regina!
Sing her praise, ye Cherubim, Join our
song, ye Seraphim!
Heav'n and earth resound the hymn:
Salve, Salve, Salve Regina!

12. DEAR GUARDIAN OF MARY

Dear Guardian of Mary,
dear nurse of her Child!
Life's ways are full weary,
the desert is wild;
Bleak sands are all 'round us.
no home can we see;
Sweet spouse of our Lady,
we lean safe on thee.

For thou to the pilgrim
art father and guide,
And Jesus and Mary
felt safe at thy side.
O Glorious Patron
secure shall I be,
Sweet spouse of our Lady,
if thou stay with me!

God chose thee for Jesus
and Mary; wilt thou
Forgive a poor exile
for choosing thee now?
There's no saint in heaven,
St. Joseph like thee,

Sweet Spouse of our Lady,
do thou plead for me.

13. AMERICA THE BEAUTIFUL

O beautiful for spacious skies,
For amber waves of grain,
For purple mountain majesties
Above the fruited plain!
America! America!
God shed his grace on thee,
And crown thy good with brotherhood
From sea to shining sea.

O beautiful for pilgrim feet,
Whose stern, impassioned stress
A thoroughfare for freedom beat
Across the wilderness!
America! America!
God mend thine ev'ry flaw,
Confirm thy soul in self-control,
Thy liberty in law.

14. GOD BLESS AMERICA

GOD BLESS AMERICA
Land that I love
Stand beside her and guide her
Thru the night with a light from above
From the mountains to the prairies
To the oceans white with foam
GOD BLESS AMERICA
My home sweet home
GOD BLESS AMERICA
My home sweet home.

78. AFC CENACLE HYMN

Alleluia, Alleluia; Alleluia, Alleluia
Alleluia, Alleluia; Alleluia, Alleluia.

I love you Father, I love you Father;
I love you Father, I love you Father.

I love you Jesus, I love you Jesus;
I love you Jesus, I love you Jesus.

I love you Spirit, I love you Spirit;
I love you Spirit, I love you Spirit.

I love you Mary, I love you Mary;
I love you Mary, I love you Mary.

I love you Joseph, I love you Joseph;
I love you Joseph, I love you Joseph.

I love you angels, I love you angels;
I love you angels, I love you angels.

I love you patrons, I love you patrons;
I love you patrons, I love you patrons.

I love you Jesus, I love you Jesus;
I love you Jesus, I love you Jesus.

I love you Jesus, I love you Jesus;
I love you Jesus, I love you Jesus.

Alleluia, Alleluia; Alleluia, Alleluia
Alleluia, Alleluia; Alleluia, Alleluia.

Reply Section

1. ( ) Please place this petition at the foot of the altar in your Sacred Hearts Chapel and include it in all of the Masses said for the needs of your petitioners throughout the coming week. Also include these petitions in your vigil of prayer on Fridays, particularly on First Fridays when your president spends his day or night before Our Eucharistic Lord praying for the intentions of all petitions received throughout the month.

_____

_____

_____

_____

_____

_____

_____

_____

_____

_____

2.a ( ) I promise to pray that God will use The Apostolate to inspire people to become instruments to renew the family and the entire world in Jesus Christ. I would like to be listed as a Sacri-State member and participate in the spiritual benefits of The Apostolate.

2b ( ) I am a priest, and will include the intentions of The Apostolate and all of those who are asking for your prayers in my available Masses, particularly on Fridays.

3. ( ) Enclosed is my best for God, my seed-Charity donation for the vital work of The Apostolate. _____

4. ( ) Enclosed is a list of names of people who should be interested in The Apostolate.

5. ( ) I am not on your mailing list, please add my name.

6. ( ) Please notify me when you start to organize chapters in my area.

7. ( ) I would like to receive more information about Cooperator membership.

8. ( ) Please send your order form for your prayer books and materials.

Please Print:

Name: _____

Address: _____

City & State: _____

Zip: _____

The Apostolate, Box 220, Kenosha, WI 53141